BALANCED
GOLF

To Kurt,

May the "Balanced"
way lend new insights
to improving your game!

Best Wishes,
Ted Kleigel 7-3-99

BALANCED GOLF

Harnessing the Simplicity, Focus, and Natural Motions of Martial Arts to Improve Your All-Around Game

TED KIEGIEL
PGA Professional and Black Belt Master

with Peter F. Stevens

CONTEMPORARY BOOKS

Library of Congress Cataloging-in-Publication Data

Kiegiel, Ted.
    Balanced golf : harnessing the simplicity, focus, and natural
motions of martial arts to improve your all-around game / Ted
Kiegiel with Peter F. Stevens.
        p.   cm.
    ISBN 0-8092-2810-6
    1. Swing (Golf).   2. Golf—Study and teaching.   3. Martial
arts—Study and teaching.   4. Movement education.   I. Stevens,
Peter F.   II. Title.
GV979.S9K54   1999
613.7'148—dc21
                               98-37061
                                  CIP

Cover design by Todd Petersen
Cover photograph copyright © Barbour Photography
Interior design by Hespenheide Design
Interior photographs by Ray Barbour, Barbour Photography

Published by Contemporary Books
A division of NTC/Contemporary Publishing Group, Inc.
4255 West Touhy Avenue, Lincolnwood (Chicago), Illinois 60646-1975 U.S.A.
Copyright © 1999 by Ted Kiegiel and Peter Stevens
Printed in the United States of America
International Standard Book Number: 0-8092-2810-6

99 00 01 02 03 04 CU 18 17 16 15 14 13 12 11 10 9 8 7 6 5 4 3 2 1

To my wife, Krissy, who has shared in all my achievements and dreams. Your unending love and support are everything to me. And to my heavenly angel—Sarah. Those above have truly blessed me.

To my family—Dad, Mom, John, and Barbara—I couldn't have accomplished any of this without you.

To my wife's family, whose years of encouragement taught me so many valuable life lessons. And to my wife's father, whom we so tragically lost some years ago. Dad, I think of you often and miss you.

To Dave Spencer and Bob Kletcke—my mentors. Thank you for giving me the opportunity of a lifetime. Because of you both, the lore of Augusta is permanently etched in my heart.

To Michael Breed, my brother in every sense of the word.

And lastly, my deepest gratitude to all the Master-Teachers who were so giving of their knowledge. Just as they have passed on the torch of Eastern mastery to me, I too will impart the knowledge to those who seek this path.

CONTENTS

PREFACE

This book represents many years of intensive study in my chosen profession—golf—and in the martial arts. I began the first half of my journey, in golf, at a young age and was determined to learn as much as possible. Moving up and down the East Coast and working for some of the most respected head professionals, I was privileged enough to work at the Augusta National Golf Club (Georgia), The Country Club (Brookline, Massachusetts), the Maidstone Club (East Hampton, New York), and the Jupiter Hills Club (Jupiter, Florida). At the same time, I had the good fortune of competing in many tournaments. Little did I know that what I was learning on the practice tee and from fellow professional golfers was leading me on my first steps to Balanced Golf.

The other half of my journey began with a second passion—the martial arts. As my training in Eastern movement and philosophy progressed, I studied in numerous dojos (martial arts academies) under several of the nation's most talented master/teachers and earned my black belt status. The deeper I immersed myself in my martial arts training, the more I began to discover physical, mental, and even emotional connections between the martial artist and the golfer. After years of blending components of the martial arts into my own golf game and discovering that my game became steadier, I realized I was onto something. That something was the start of my system— Balanced Golf, a combination of traditional Western golf techniques and martial arts techniques.

Once I began teaching my method, the improvement in my students' games was nothing less than extraordinary. They shaved strokes off their handicaps, and their enjoyment of the game increased. Balanced Golf can do the same for you.

This book presents my system in two sections. Part I, Getting on the Path of Balanced Golf, isolates each key segment of your swing's sequence by looking first at the classical Western instructional tradition and then introducing you to the simple Eastern principles, techniques, and exercises that will balance your swing permanently with incredible accuracy and power.

Part II, Staying on the Path of Balanced Golf, shows you how to develop and maintain the proper blend of East and West. Together, both sections address your swing from a truly revolutionary perspective.

I know that when some people hear the words "martial arts," images of kicks and punches come to mind. Let me assure you right from the start that there will be none of that whatsoever. You're not going to learn self-defense here. However, you're going to learn how to defend your swing against every enemy: poor posture, faulty impact, hooks, slices, and so on.

Much of the book's subject matter has never been applied or addressed in this manner until now. Balanced Golf offers you the martial arts' truth in natural movement and gives you the tools to develop a fluid golf swing. As you find incredible harmony and power from the East in your swing, you'll also discover something else: in all aspects of daily life, you'll move better and have an easier time focusing.

A famous martial arts master once said, "True knowledge is self-knowledge, and self-knowledge is a lifelong process." Balanced Golf is my lifelong process, and I want to share its basic secrets with you. All you have to do is clear your mind of any preconceptions about the martial arts and read on. The best swing of your life—the swing *for* your lifetime—awaits you.

INTRODUCTION
WHEN EAST MEETS WEST

"How can they make something so hard look so easy?" In my years as a PGA professional and instructor from the Augusta National Golf Club to the Carolina Country Club, hundreds of my golf students have asked me this question. I have had the chance to study the classic swings of Greg Norman, Raymond Floyd, Fred Couples, Mac O'Grady, and many other Tour golfers up close and personal. "You know what?" I answer my pupils. "It's not easy, and a good swing only comes with practice and sound fundamentals."

I also tell my students something else. I can show them the way to a more fluid and powerful swing, the one they dream about. I can reveal the secrets and the techniques that will have them playing the best golf of their lives. Even better, I can show them how to do it consistently, every round.

What's my system's secret? I take the best of the traditional swing and "marry" it to basic martial arts principles and exercises. When I open your mind to the Eastern half of your game, your Western half will be a perfect complement. You'll mold a perfect swing shape, which will give you the confidence to shoot low rounds.

Before I introduce you to the Eastern half of your swing, I have to admit that I began my journey to Balanced Golf on the traditional Western path. I learned the same swing keys from setup to finish that you have. "Keep your left arm straight" and "don't move your head"—these principles were drilled into me by my first instructors. One of them had a teaching method I didn't enjoy much. To keep my head still, he held my hair as I swung the club. You'll be happy to know that this technique has no place in my book.

As I put in more practice sessions than I can remember during my teens, I climbed up the ladder of tough junior golf competition. By the mid-1980s, I had earned my PGA Class A-1 status. My years of studying and practicing the traditional Western swing were paying off. I now began taking advantage of the opportunity to study the games of Greg Norman, Raymond Floyd, and other PGA Tour players from the best possible vantage point—near them at the range or during their practice rounds before the Masters, the U.S. Open, and other Tour events. I watched Greg Norman's power, Freddie Couples's "soft hands," Raymond Floyd's determination, and Mac O'Grady's virtuoso swing. Believe me, even though I have stood next to these guys, I'm as astonished by their swings as anyone else.

In my early PGA years, I analyzed those great swings through my Western view. But I was slowly coming to another understanding that went far beyond the traditional approach. I was looking at the game from an Eastern angle—with good reason. I had become a serious student of the martial arts.

As a twelve-year-old, about the same time I committed myself to golf, I enrolled in a martial arts program. At that time, the Bruce Lee films were quite popular, and I have to admit they served as an inspiration for me. Although my parents weren't too thrilled with the idea of letting me learn "exotic" kicks and punches, I finally wore them down. When they realized that my classes were about discipline rather than violence, they supported my new passion as much as my other one (golf).

As I continued my martial arts training, I learned about the Asian principles of *natural law*. These are the forces that rule everyone's body and mind. Within the teachings of natural law, I learned the principles of *yin* (yield) and *yang* (force) and of *ki*, the "One-Point" from where I could summon reserves of power and emotional strength. From my studies with several of America's most famous martial arts masters, I learned that the natural law of body alignments and body rotation direct countless movements on and off the martial arts mat.

As those experts in Asian techniques patiently shared their wisdom with me, I had plenty of time to think about their theories each time I was tossed to the mat. But I stuck with it. Today, twenty years later, I have attained a Master Level ranking with black belts in various systems and run my own dojo.

When my martial arts journey began, I didn't make the connection between the dojo and the golf course right away. Both were still separate disciplines to me. But with continuous training, my skills matured, and I began to realize that natural law must also govern the golf swing. Why? Because it governs all physical movement, whether it's golf or any other athletic motion.

I began to experiment by using simple martial arts techniques in my own golf game. They calmed my nerves at tournaments, keeping those inner demons at bay. Using several easy breathing routines steadied me over the ball. Once I was relaxed, it made it quite easy for me to use the yielding power of yin and the explosive force of yang in my takeaway and backswing. The exchanging process of energy in my swing worked every time, and soon my skill level rose even further.

Then I began to study the swings of world-class players, but this time with my Eastern view. At Augusta, just before the 1988

Masters, I watched Greg Norman hit every shot hard. His unique talent allowed him to do this with control, but for normal golfers his personal technique would be disastrous. Why? Because they would mimic him and swing harder. As I watched Greg up close, I found that his power flowed from the same natural body alignments that the martial arts teach. I realized that through natural law, any golfer could similarly align his or her own body and receive tremendous results.

From Freddie Couples before the 1992 Masters, I also learned a key lesson in how the martial arts applied to a golf swing. In a practice round, I noticed that Freddie's relaxed stance and limbs triggered the smooth and powerful swing that had earned him the affectionate nickname "Boom-Boom." I saw that he swung the club with no rigid joints. On one particularly difficult up-and-down shot, his hands and fingers held his wedge so softly that his right hand actually came off the grip on his follow-through, and his ball still rolled within a few inches of the cup. Relaxation for results—a key principle of natural law.

One of the most important lessons I learned in natural law was during a round I played at the Augusta National Golf Club with Mac O'Grady, a close friend and a valued swing coach for many Tour professionals. As we stood in the middle of the 13th fairway, Mac dropped four balls at the 200-yard marker. The hole is shaped as a dogleg left with a creek running in front of the entire green—a challenging par-5 to say the least. Mac stepped up to his first ball with a 4-iron and cracked his shot dead onto the green. To my surprise, he then reached for his 5-iron and smacked a second ball onto the green. I swear that my jaw dropped as he fired his third ball near the cup with a 6-iron. What could I do except shake my head in disbelief when he swung his 7-iron and—you've got it—dropped the ball onto the green.

Four different clubs hit the same distance! How could anyone do that? After some pondering, my martial arts training revealed the only possible answer. Mac's personal mastery of body alignments and grounding allowed him to increase his torso's rotational speed without throwing him off balance. Again, the martial arts opened the door of knowledge and gave me a valuable key.

The time had arrived to put my "marriage" of basic martial arts principles and the Western golf swing to the test. I was already taking students through the key Western swing steps—setup, backswing, transition/downswing, impact, follow-through, and finish. What my students did not yet know was that I had been teaching them these traditional positions with a "twist"—fundamental ideas of natural law—using the principles of yin and yang, ki, joint rounding, and body alignments. When my pupils began striking all of their woods and irons straighter and longer, I told them my secret. They were amazed that simple Eastern techniques were healing their Western swing flaws. I explained to them that natural law directs all golfers from Tiger Woods to the beginner, and that basic martial arts principles and an open mind were the ways to Balanced Golf.

Many of my students were now convinced, but I knew that some fellow professionals might be skeptical unless I provided "documented" evidence that my system really worked. I recruited two members from the Carolina Country Club to act as my golfing "guinea pigs." I told them my experiment would last one month and consist of four lessons. First, I taught them a series of simple martial arts exercises that they performed five to seven times a week. They found the basic breathing routines of ki and the stance and turning techniques easy and fun. Once a week I took them through practice-tee sessions and applied the Eastern exercises to their traditional and erratic Western swings. I videotaped each session. The film didn't lie—the dramatic improvement in both students' swings was there for anyone to see. Both had made significant improvement in only four weeks. These two golfers were playing Balanced Golf for the first time, and my simple martial arts approach had unlocked their natural powers. They now had the tools to keep their swings on target and had acquired these tools by opening their minds to the East.

Having proved that my unique system would shape a sound basic swing, I next set out to blend other Western and Eastern approaches to solve specific problems. I customized drills, techniques, and simple exercises that truly ironed out problems by combining East and West.

I can show you how to find the path to Balanced Golf, as I have shown hundreds of my students. You'll be amazed at the hidden reservoir of physical and emotional power within you. All you have to do is follow the "guidepost"—natural law. I can show you how yin and yang, ki, earth power, body alignments, and other principles of the East will balance your game for life if you stick with the system.

The martial arts can revolutionize your game from the ground up. But you must be willing to practice what the lessons in this book preach. If you accept the challenge, natural law will lead you to the proficiency, power, and consistency all golfers seek—Balanced Golf.

It's time for East to meet West in your golf game.

BALANCED
GOLF

PART 1

GETTING ON THE PATH OF BALANCED GOLF

1

THE SETUP—
YOUR BALANCING ACT

Most golfers underestimate the importance of their setup. In theory, the setup is the simplest part of the game. But, as I've seen over and over with new students, they do something wrong the moment they step up to the ball. Without a proper setup, no one can make a proper swing.

From the moment a professional-caliber player sets up over the ball, he aligns his head, limbs, torso, and legs in a balanced posture. He is primed before the club has even moved, and it's no accident that his takeaway and backswing look so smooth and effortless. His setup has freed him for balanced power.

Before I reveal the martial arts principles that will cure your setup for good, we need to take a quick refresher course in how the Western setup looks and feels. First, we will cover the steps needed to establish a repeatable routine and then apply basic Eastern techniques to ensure a perfectly balanced setup for your takeaway.

THE WESTERN SETUP

When I'm working with a student, I first analyze his setup from my Western point of view, listing the flaws that will disrupt optimum balance and power. The most common errors I see fall into one or more of the following categories:

- Knee flex
- Waist bend
- Arms
- Head tilt
- Shoulder tilt
- Width of stance

FIGURE 1.1 SETUP, DRIVER—FRONT VIEW

FIGURE 1.2 SETUP, DRIVER—SIDE VIEW

- Foot flare
- Swing center
- Weight distribution
- Ball placement
- Grip
- Hand position

This section gives a rundown of the traditional Western basics with which any golfer needs to be familiar before stepping onto the Eastern path of Balanced Golf.

Knee Flex

You must bend your knees slightly and comfortably. Because the knee is a ball-and-socket joint, you'll feel tightness in it if you turn it inward or outward improperly at setup.

Waist Bend

After you have addressed the ball, you should bend forward from your waist just enough to feel athletic and comfortable. The right amount will afford your upper body its proper freedom of movement. You'll know the appropriate amount instinctively—it's the one that's comfortable, the one in which you feel no muscle tension.

Arms

The ideal setup position for your arms is at a slight angle away from your body. This will automatically prime them for the correct swing path. You must also be aware of any tension in your arms. It's a myth that you must maintain a rigid straight left arm—just relax and soften up your joints so that your energy can flow.

Head Tilt

This seems like a gimme. However, I work with a number of students who either "lock" their heads at setup or have their head tilted abnormally.

Your head should bend downward slightly, and your chin should be aligned with the center of your body. You should also feel no stiffness in your neck at all. Once we take our first steps down the Eastern path, you'll discover a few martial arts techniques that will unlock your head at setup so you can encourage a fluid swing.

Shoulder Tilt

For a right-handed golfer at setup, the ideal position is for the right shoulder to be slightly lower than the left. This will ensure the proper trajectory for all your shots. Level shoulders will produce a lower to medium ball flight and, for most players, that's a difficult shot pattern to manage.

Width of Stance

If you set up too wide, your weight shift and body rotation will be obstructed; too narrow and your upper torso takes over, destroying your balance.

Determining the width of your stance gets even more complicated because club selection demands adjustments in your stance. For your driver, you'll set up in your widest stance. In this case, the inside of your feet should measure to the outside of your shoulders. From this position, the distance shortens with each lower yardage club, until you are taking your narrowest stances with your short irons (9 through sand wedge). At this point, the outside of your feet should measure to the outside of your shoulders. You can see and feel that a natural narrowing process has taken place.

Foot Flare

Your right foot should flare outward two to three inches. This allows you to keep your weight on the inside of your right leg in the backswing and prevents your knee from turning outward.

Your left foot should point four to five inches toward the left. Now your hips are capable of turning 45 degrees in your backswing.

Some golf observers might challenge this setup of the left foot. "What about Lee Trevino?" they may ask. "His left foot flares outward much farther." That's true. But you must be aware of the limitations this position causes. For one, you can't turn your hips as far in the backswing. This alone will change a golfer's swing shape. For that reason, I strongly urge you to stick with the four- to five-inch flare.

Swing Center

At setup, your center is simply an imaginary straight line that bisects your body from head to toe. This is an important ingredient in your setup because it ultimately dictates how your club will strike the ball. For each club in your bag, these approximate center positions apply:

> Driver and fairway woods—
> Seven inches behind ball
> 2-, 3-, and 4-irons—Three
> inches behind ball
> 5-, 6-, and 7-irons—One inch
> behind ball
> 8-iron to sand wedge—Directly
> on ball

Although these are the classic center positions, you can modify them slightly to accommodate your own height, weight, and frame.

Weight Distribution

For woods, your weight should favor the right side slightly—55 percent on the right leg, 45 percent on the left. This will increase your chances of striking the ball just as the club is moving upward at impact.

For your irons, position your weight equally on each leg to aid a downward angle of attack.

Ball Placement

There are two schools of thought on ball placement in your setup. Some players, including Jack Nicklaus, use the one-ball-position method. This means that for any given club, the ball is placed just inside the left heel.

The second method, which I prefer for students, uses a variety of placements. I feel that by adjusting the ball from the center of your stance to the left heel area, you have much better control over the angle of attack for each club.

Grip

The grip is your one connection to the golf club, so it has to be done

correctly and should feel comfortable. In addition, a good or bad grip directly affects how your wrists will function throughout the swing. If your hands are positioned correctly (fig. 1.3), they encourage your wrists to do a simple but crucial job: hinge the club in the backswing and unhinge it in the downswing. That's it.

I advise you to maintain a slightly strong grip. This is when your left hand is positioned more clockwise on the club. It's been my experience that players with a neutral or weak grip tend to manipulate the club too much. This creates added movement to the clubface and is just another troubling segment of your swing to be monitored.

There are more rules for your grip that cannot be violated. First, the strength from your hands is in your fingers. If you were to pick up a bucket of water, you wouldn't place the handle in the palm of your hand; you would naturally grab it with your fingers and lift the bucket. Second, both hands must move together as a unit. Don't allow them to oppose each other in any way. That usually happens when they separate—so keep them together. Also, your palms should face each other, regardless of

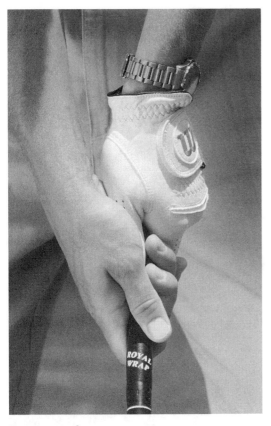

FIGURE 1.3 GRIP—FRONT VIEW

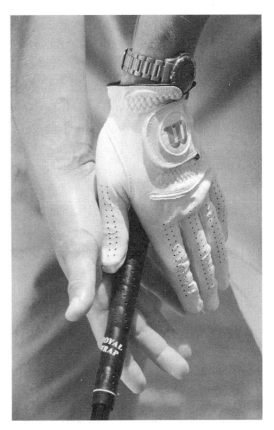

FIGURE 1.4 GRIP WITH OPEN HANDS—FRONT VIEW

whether you have a strong or weak grip.

To test yourself, hold onto a club with your usual grip. Now, open your fingers with both hands and extend them (fig. 1.4). At this point, your palms should face each other.

From this point, let's start with the placement of your left hand. The grip end of your club should rest along the bottoms of your fin-gers. When closing your hand, the heel pad should rest on top of your grip. Your hand should be turned slightly clockwise from a neutral position.

As far as your right hand is con-cerned, you want the center of your right palm, or the life line, resting on the top portion of your left thumb. The fingers of your right hand should hold the club as do those of your left hand, at the base of your fingers. The palm of your right hand must mirror the palm of your left hand.

The pinky of your right hand can be placed either on top of or intertwined with the index finger of your left hand. This forms either an overlapping or interlocking grip, respectively. These two grips are most commonly used. If you lack hand strength, the ten-finger base-ball grip is acceptable as long as your hands don't separate during the swing.

Lastly, the better player may consider using the right index finger position. For this grip, it's important to have a slight gap—approximately one inch—between the right index finger and the middle finger. This placement allows you to feel the clubface position more accurately throughout the swing and is some-thing of a Tour secret. You can begin to feel this feedback after some continuous practice.

Hand Position

The ideal position for iron shots is to have your hands in line with or just slightly ahead of the ball (fig. 1.5). When you're setting up for wood shots, your hands should be just behind the ball (fig. 1.6).

FIGURE 1.5 SETUP WITH HANDS IN FRONT OF BALL, 6-IRON—FRONT VIEW

FIGURE 1.6 SETUP WITH HANDS BEHIND BALL, DRIVER—FRONT VIEW

If your hands are set too far forward, you will hinge your wrists too quickly in the backswing and create a very sharp angle of attack. On the other hand, if your hands are too far behind the ball, you must make significant adjustments to the path of your club.

The Eastern Half

Now that we have gone over the Western setup's basics, it's time to meet the Eastern guides that will reveal what traditional golf lessons lack: martial arts principles and techniques that allow you to set up perfectly balanced each and every time. Welcome to your first step.

Yin and Yang— Two Halves of a Whole

Anything that disrupts your setup's yin will wreck your takeaway's yang.

"My what?" is my new students' usual response.

Yin and yang—these two opposing but linked forces rule all movement. Asian cultures define them as "the universal balance of life."

That's probably great in the dojo, you're thinking, but what's the point for a golfer? The key word here is balance—the balance that yin and yang bring to your swing. Although I could give you long, detailed lessons in the mystical Eastern philosophies of yin and yang, my Balanced Golf system sticks to clear, simple explanations of these two forces and their connection to your swing.

As I have mentioned, there are many Eastern definitions of yin and yang. In China, it is believed that yin is nature's passive energy and that yang is forceful energy. For golfers, I simply define these forces as the two states of energy that control every movement. *Yin* is any motion that yields. It occurs immediately before and after a movement with any degree of force, or *yang*. If you reach for a light switch, your arm and fingers move with a small measure of force. When you pull away from the switch, the force recedes to a relaxed state. That means yang (force) has given way to yin (yield).

Let's use an example that all golfers have experienced. To remove your clubs from the car trunk, you first place your hand on your golf bag's strap. At this moment, your arm is set up in a state of yin, ready to yield to the force necessary to lift the bag. As you lift it, you apply the correct amount of force, or yang. Now, as you place your bag on the ground, the force you've used ebbs naturally as your body yields again to yin.

Although you have never realized it, the principle of yin and yang is crucial to your golf game because it controls every part of your swing. When you set up over the ball, you assume a state of yin. Yang begins with your backswing. As your backswing ends, you reach the most crucial moment—the yin transition to your downswing. At this instant, your swing shifts again to a yang condition. Yang continues through your downswing, and you finish your swing in a yin state. The proper sequence of yield and force is created in this manner:

> Setup—Yin
> Backswing—Yang
> Top of backswing to
>   transition—Yin
> Downswing, impact, and
>   follow-through—Yang
> Finish—Yin

Whether on the practice range or in my dojo, nothing works better than hands-on lessons and examples. So, for your first lesson in Balanced Golf—martial arts and your setup—put yourself in my students' shoes as we head to the course.

First, I'd like you to walk up to a practice tee. Guess what? Yin and yang just guided your movements. When you headed to the tee, you yielded one leg from a state of yin, or setup, and shifted it into a state of yang, or force. Whenever you're in motion, any motion, your body moves from yin to yang again and again. Now that you're at the tee, stop for a moment. Your body relaxes. It yields to yin.

You tee up a ball and take your usual Western setup. If I lean my hand against the side of your right shoulder, you feel your weight shift to the left. When I push against your left shoulder, your weight shifts to the right. Then, I press against your chest and next your back. If your stance is disturbed at any point, you have no stability.

Again, you ask, "What's the point of this?" If your shoulders, your torso, your head, your grip, or anything else is even slightly off at setup, you *can't* swing the club correctly. You *can't* move effectively into the backswing's yang if your setup's yin has been disturbed. I use this same lesson in the dojo—without a 5-iron, of course.

During my journey to black belt status, one of my masters/teachers said, "The outstanding characteristic of the expert athlete is his or her ease of movement." This epitomizes the yin and yang theory. Fluid movement comes only if a relaxed state of yin yields in a smooth transition to the forceful motions of yang. If you have ever played a links course, you have been near a perfect example of yin and yang. As waves gather offshore, they set up in a state of yin. Then, as the water surges forward and crashes against the beach, it creates the force of yang. When the water recedes, it again returns to yin. Over and over, the waves ebb and flow with yin and yang.

The problem for most golfers is that their swings' physical barriers strip away the balance and power of yin and yang. Think about what happens when waves surge against a sea wall. This man-made obstacle disrupts the waves' force, or yang, by preventing the surf from surging to its farthest natural distance. It breaks up the water's power.

Golfers break up their swings at setup the same way. Maybe it's a knee turned inward or outward, a foot flared too wide, or a waist that doesn't squarely face the ball. These physical obstacles disrupt the setup's yin and fuel poor transitions to yang in the backswing, in the downswing, and at impact. Loss of power, erratic swing path, faulty weight transfer, hooks, slices, and many other errors result from the violations of yin and yang. But if you obey the natural exchange of yin and yang energy, it will serve you well.

Let the Horse Be Your Guide

A simple martial arts stance called the Horse is the foundation of many moves I teach in my dojo. This ancient stance places you in the perfect golfing setup (fig. 1.7). To do this, you simply follow these steps:

1. Spread your feet apart.
2. Lean forward slightly at your waist, and slightly flex your knees.

3. With your head forward and your spine erect, point your fingers at the floor with your thumbs resting against the outside of your thighs.

FIGURE 1.7 HORSE STANCE—FRONT VIEW

What does this simple stance do for your game? It does plenty. The Horse won't let you turn your knees and feet too far inward or outward: they are exactly where they should be in the golf setup. Put my words to the test by trying to turn a knee or foot just a little bit while you are in the Horse stance. You feel a sudden tension not only in the area you're turning, but also in your waist. You feel tight and constricted. The Horse is telling you that your setup's unbalanced and that you're primed for a flawed backswing.

Set up in the Horse stance again, spreading your feet to shoulder width and slightly flexing your knees. Take a look at your waist now. It is positioned so that when you pick up a club, they will be parallel to the target line and squarely facing the ball. Your stance for takeaway is perfect.

In three simple, repeatable steps, the Horse has brought basic yin into your golf stance. If you follow the Horse, you *can't* misalign your head, knees, waist, and feet at setup. If you feel any hint that your regular setup is off, all you have to do is back off the ball and use the Horse to reset yourself perfectly.

With your Horse stance in place, we can bring the dojo's natural laws of body alignments and earth power to your setup for more power and control.

The Natural Laws of Body Alignments and Joint Rounding

The martial arts teach that nature has engineered the human body for fluid, effective movement. In the dojo, I've learned and taught that only if we obey the natural law of body alignments can we tap our bodies' full balance and power. One of the foundations in natural law is that correct body alignments will create maximum balance and power from minimal effort. To align ourselves properly for any motion, we must focus upon four areas:

- Head
- Torso
- Lower body
- Arms

In its simplest definition, the *natural law of body alignments* tells us that if one of the four key areas is positioned incorrectly at a given movement, the other three can't do their job properly. I will reveal the Eastern alignments that will give you the perfect setup shortly, but you might be surprised to know that you've already mastered natural law in many of your daily actions. When you get behind the wheel of your car, you don't grab the steering wheel with both hands on one side. If you do, you're hampering your ability to drive. Typically, you will align your arms in the most comfortable position for maximum control of the wheel. Similarly, when you're in the kitchen and have to reach across your body for a pan or a glass of water, you turn your entire torso rather than just moving your arms and straining yourself. Having performed the actions so many times, you repeat them instinctively. You obey natural law by aligning your body to carry out the task—no more and no less than is necessary.

When I prepare for a strike in the dojo, I align my head, arms, torso, and legs in the precise manner that will allow me to launch a punch or kick with minimal effort and maximum effect. You won't be throwing punches in Balanced Golf, of course, but their example does lead us from the dojo back to the practice range. The connection? The alignments with which martial artists set up strikes show golfers how to engineer their bodies for the perfect setup to the takeaway and backswing.

Natural law supplies maximum balance and power from a relaxed state—power flow like a waterfall. In the dojo, this principle requires you to "round" your joints. By *joint rounding*, I refer to a slight, comfortable bend in your joints. Rigid, or locked, joints are the ultimate enemy of most golf swings. I have learned that most golfers start joint locking at their setup. I speak from personal experience here. Until the martial arts taught me that stiff limbs were not a strength but a weakness in alignments, I didn't realize that most golfers who strained to keep their left arm straight tightened up everywhere.

When I was a kid eagerly learning the game, my instructors taught me the traditional Western swing with its immobile head and rigid arm positions. You will probably recall my previous mention of the golf teacher who held me by my hair to prevent any movement. I can sum up this type of thinking in one word: Ouch! As my understanding of various Asian systems increased, I saw how rigid joints violated natural law. In the dojo, I had the bruises to prove it. But I still wasn't quite ready to unlock my setup and backswing. After all, I didn't want to mess with the success my Western swing had brought me. Still, I began to study just how rigid the setups and swings of Nick Price, Greg Norman, Ray Floyd, and other PGA professionals were.

At the same time, I found myself looking at the stances and movements of athletes in other sports. I was searching for proof that natural law ruled them. I found it. For example, I noticed that Tony Gwynn, the great San Diego Padres hitter, sets up in the batter's box—his yin state—and literally swings into his yang state as the ball leaves the pitcher's hand. From setup through swing, Gwynn's eyes are focused on the ball, but his head is not rigid. As his bat connects with the ball, his head comes off the ball ever so slightly. His head moves—and it should.

Maybe you've heard tennis broadcasters who have said that Pete Sampras and Martina Hingis lock their heads and "watch" the ball come off their rackets. Well, guess what? The moment those rackets make contact and the follow-through begins, a player's head and eyes come off the ball. Their heads move.

I'm not going to teach you to let your head flop around as you move from setup to swing. I am stating flat out that you don't have to lock your head into place at setup and that you can move your head slightly—several inches to the right in the backswing and roughly twice that amount to the left during the downswing. In the dojo, similar movements help prevent rigidity in strikes and counterstrikes; on the golf course, freeing your head to move slightly similarly allows your upper torso and your lower body to link in a smooth, balanced swing. This unlocking process must begin at setup.

In my dojo, my newest students make the mistake of "freezing" their joints as they set up in a stance. I have found the same problem among my newest golf pupils. As they set up on the practice tee, they're thinking "keep the head steady and the left arm locked." Many have already been taught the Western view that a golf swing with solid rotation around a fixed axis, with the head or sternum acting as the pivot point, will provide the most effective results. Pure rotation does generate the most solid shots. But such rotation is only suitable for machines such as the "Iron Byron" robots that golf equipment companies use to test balls and state-of-the-art shafts and club-heads. Nature did not construct the human body—not even that of Greg Norman or Tiger Woods—to match the rotation of Iron Byron. If you're too stiff at setup, you're already producing body tension that will invade your swing. You're violating natural law before you have even begun your takeaway. As soon as you start your takeaway, your rigid joints begin to destroy your swing in two clear ways:

- Poor kinetic power (energy release), robbing your shots of distance and accuracy
- Terrible balance, setting the stage for hooks, slices, and any number of other flaws

"So, where does joint lockup occur most?" ask my martial arts students and golf students alike. My answer is the head, the neck, the shoulders, the elbows, the wrists, the fingers, the hips, the knees, the ankles, and the feet—in short, everywhere.

The fingers can pose a particular problem. Often, when I ask new pupils to show me their normal setup, they think they're relaxed—until I tell them to feel their grip. Their fingers are literally choking the club, impeding their timing and rhythm and creating added tension throughout the upper torso. The tension spreads up the forearms, surges into the shoulders, and stiffens the neck and chest. They're primed for a rigid swing deprived of power and balance.

It sounds discouraging, but it's not—not if you start to unlock your joints at setup. Since the setup is the primer for the backswing, your stance over the ball must be correct at that moment to trigger the shift from yin to yang.

Once again, a look outside golf is helpful here. As in golf, the setups in other sports fuel the athletes' motions. If you watch the premier server in tennis, Pete Sampras, at the instant before his serve's toss, you will note his perfectly relaxed posture from head to toe, about to explode into a 120-MPH shot. Even for Sampras, a locked joint can result in a serve smashing into the top of the net or kicking a yard past the white line.

If you enjoy baseball, take a look at Toronto's Roger Clemens and Atlanta's Greg Maddux. They relax on the pitching mound an instant before kicking into their windups. Both pitchers set up with their bodies aligned and their joints relaxed. Their setups allow them to release their natural energy and power without strain.

I will give you one more example from another sport. When Dallas Cowboy quarterback Troy Aikman crouches behind the center or steps back into the shotgun formation, are his arms rigid? Are his knees stiff? Certainly not—he's in a relaxed stance, yin, and will shift into yang to throw a tight spiral downfield.

Now, let's get back to the practice tee. At this point, most of my students are intrigued by my challenge to the rigid swing. Some pose one more question. It's a good one and goes something like this: Why can many PGA Tour players such as Paul Azinger tighten their joints and be successful? My answer is that the success of famous rigid swingers hinges on their personal traits, years of practice, and, as my

friend Mac O'Grady says, "the God-given talent of the virtuoso." If life were fair, we could all drive the ball like John Daly or Tiger Woods, but no one—not even other PGA Tour players—can.

The fact is that for every successful rigid swinger on Tour, many more prefer the relaxed condition of joint rounding. It works for them, and it works for hundreds of my students. It will work for you because it's only natural, and natural law is what Balanced Golf is all about.

To loosen you up for a correct setup, I have a simple stance and a basic exercise from my dojo. Both will relax you and align your limbs and torso for a proper golf stance.

The Stack

This basic stance, called the Stack (fig. 1.8), is a key step in properly aligning your setup. The way to achieve this stance is simple:

1. Stand with your arms hanging loosely and with your palms comfortably facing your thighs.
2. Relax your shoulders, arms, torso, legs, and feet; you'll feel a sensation that they are pulling downward.

3. With your head level and your spine erect, I want you to feel a sense of flexibility—rounding—from head to toe.

4. You are now stacked for a relaxed setup.

How has this primed you for a relaxed setup? By aligning your stance and fully relaxing, you have eliminated the tension throughout your body. Because your fingers are hanging loosely in this stance, your

FIGURE 1.8 STACK
STANCE—FRONT VIEW

arms and shoulders are loose. Your arms are extended, as they must be in your swing, but they're relaxed. You have rounded and relaxed your joints. That's what rounding is: loosening your joints so that tension can't distress your setup and backswing. In the dojo, I compare this absence of tension to the image of a garden hose. Even though a hose may be full of water ready to burst from the nozzle, the hose itself remains completely pliable. A martial artist and a golfer alike must have this pliable alignment before they move from the setup's yin to the backswing's yang.

This alignment stacks your setup—you have "engineered" your torso and lower body for perfect balance over the ball. Because you have relaxed your hands, arms, shoulders, legs, and feet, you have stacked both your upper and lower body for smooth movement into the takeaway. How do you know whether you're stacked properly? You can feel it: the downward sensation of all your limbs in this stance tells you that you're aligning yourself correctly. When you feel this type of posture on the course, you have stacked your setup for a fluid exchange of yin and yang throughout the stroke.

By practicing the Stack both at home and on the course, you'll relax your setup and, like a garden hose at the instant before the water flows with smooth and controlled force, you'll fill your setup with maximum power flow.

The Swing

A basic martial arts exercise called the Swing also allows you to chase away any undue stiffness in your setup. In the dojo, this exercise loosens your limbs for any technique; on the course, it relaxes and rounds your joints before or even when you step up to the ball. For golfers, the added beauty is that you can use it on the course without your playing partners even suspecting that it's a martial arts exercise. To do it:

1. Assume the Stack position with feet spread shoulder width; shoulders, arms, torso, legs, and feet relaxed. Your spine should be erect and your head level (fig. 1.9a).
2. Slowly twist your body to the left, allowing your arms to

swing freely (fig. 1.9b–
fig. 1.9c).

3. Slowly twist to the right, again
with your arms swinging freely
(fig. 1.9d–fig. 1.9e).

In this exercise, you will feel
your head rotate naturally with your
body's left and right turns. Also, you
will feel that your weight doesn't
shift from side to side as you swing.
Your head, arms, shoulders, and
lower torso move fluidly.

What you're doing is taking the
Stack one step further by adding the

A

B

C

FIGURE 1.9 THE SWING—FRONT VIEW

D

E

Swing exercise. This exercise helps you to round your joints, eliminate a rigid head position, and soften up your limbs and torso. As with the Stack, you will need to practice the Swing on a regular basis.

The Stack and Swing will also help you round your elbows at setup. If the outside edge of your left elbow faces toward your target at setup, that's good. However, if the outside of your elbow faces your upper torso and the inner part is facing the ball, you are in trouble. Your setup is rigid and will guarantee a flawed impact, a hook or a slice, you get the picture. If you practice the Horse, the Stack, and the Swing, you will relax your elbows naturally—every time.

You will also discover that by using these exercises, you will relax your grip at setup. The joint-rounding effect they give you will relax your fingers on the club. Your grip should be light at address; this encourages relaxed arms. If your pressure is too tight, it locks up your entire body. Your grip pressure must increase naturally during your swing. If you're not conscious of the change in force, you're doing it right. Since your grip pressure should begin at setup with enough softness to allow for a smooth, gradual increase as you swing, you must control the energy in your hands. If you're squeezing the club, you will reduce the power in your swing because you're really going slower with tense muscles.

Put your Eastern guides to the test. Go through your exercises several times, pick up a club, and go into your setup. Feel that? Your fingers are gripping the club firmly, but with no strain. Now you have the keys to soften them every time you set up.

Earth Power—Grounding

In introducing you to the Horse, the Stack, and the Swing, I have started you on the path to a perfectly balanced, tension-free setup. Now, you're ready for the next step. Known in the dojo as earth power, *grounding* allows your feet to remain stable at setup. If you are moving around the ball like you are on a dance floor, your setup will fall apart. You are disturbing your stance's yin condition by violating a natural law—grounding. Because the martial arts teach that power comes from the ground up, you are breaking your connection when your feet move all around the ball at setup.

As with yin and yang, earth power is a complex Eastern concept. For golfers, however, it translates to the setup in two words: posture and balance. A stable stance at setup gives you the firm base you need for balance and power, and a basic martial arts approach allows you to absorb and connect with the power source literally at your feet.

Let's return to the dojo for a moment. When I discussed the Stack, I mentioned the downward sensation it gives a golfer's limbs. This was your introduction to grounding. A truly secure posture provides the feeling that all of your weight is flowing toward your feet. The Horse, the Stack, and the Swing round your joints for that downward flow, but let's take this sensation a step further through a technique that I use for my beginning martial arts students:

1. Extend your arms straight out, shoulder level.
2. Imagine that the underside of your arms is being pulled downward. It helps some students to close their eyes here.
3. After a few seconds, you will feel your arms growing heavier. If you don't strain at the first

hint of a downward pull, you will feel that you can actually relax them without lowering them. It will take several awkward-feeling attempts, but stick with it. Even with your arms fully exended, you can relax your arms.

Again, you're probably thinking it all sounds great for the dojo's stances, but what about the golf setup? Because earth power plants you on the ground with perfect balance to execute any motion, it allows you to move from your setup's yin to your backswing's yang without missing a step. After you ground your stance by allowing your weight to flow downward, you can turn loose your backswing with an incredible power surge from the ground up. You can only do this if your feet are dug in at setup. By "dug in," I don't mean rigid. I mean comfortably rooted and balanced. If you open your refrigerator door and reach for a can of soda, the movement doesn't require that you stiffen your feet and toes. There's simply no need to cause your body to react that way. Natural law dictates that all you have to do is keep your feet rooted. In my dojo, I would never

fire an effective kick or punch if my feet were all tensed up. It's the same for your golf swing.

Ki—Solid as a Mountain

"Take a deep breath and relax." We've all heard it many times. It's almost always good advice. *Almost* always—because in the golf setup, a deep breath at the wrong moment will ruin your stance's grounding, its connection to earth power.

How can a simple breath harm your setup? You can feel the answer yourself. Pick up one of your clubs, and take your usual setup. Now, take a deep breath. Your upper torso and shoulders have risen with the inhalation. In most of your everyday life, this isn't a problem, but if you move from your golf setup to your takeaway at this instant, your connection to earth power is disrupted. Your takeaway will be flawed, because your upper torso and shoulders have become top-heavy and will remain that way until you exhale.

If you begin your takeaway as you inhale, an upward surge is produced, and this can easily cause unwanted problems. Specifically, expanding your lungs just as you start your backswing can lift your shoulders and your club higher than you want. Chances are you won't be able to readjust before impact. Two basic martial arts techniques, discussed later in this section, can cure this condition permanently.

I have seen another type of ill-timed breath ruin the setup, and not just that of amateurs. Nervousness, excitement, anxiety, and frustration—all of these emotions can cause a negative rush of adrenaline that causes golfers to breathe erratically. A disruption to your breathing pattern can cause top-heaviness with each inhalation and a downward surge with each exhalation. The downward surge is not the relaxed pull of earth power, but an abrupt, stance-shattering force. It jars your connection to earth power. Your setup is unbalanced, and your backswing will be faulty. All of these errors come from incorrect breathing.

We can go back to the dojo and fix these problems. Martial artists know that controlling their breath during strikes and parries is critical to the balance and power of each movement. On the mat, if students become top-heavy when preparing for a technique, they open themselves up to a perfectly balanced opponent's kick or strike.

In the Japanese martial arts, a system of study called *ki principles* offers your setup basic breathing drills that I will reveal shortly. In its broadest sense, ki teaches that we can gather all physical and mental energy at a "balance center" in our bodies. Our breathing patterns are part of this energy. For a golfer at setup, basic ki principles are crucial because they train us to breathe in a way that won't disrupt the setup.

What's so different about ki breathing techniques is that they not only focus on filling your lungs and diaphragm at the right moment, but also on your *one-point*, a spot two inches below your navel. In Eastern thought, your one-point is the very center of your body. It is the point from which all your power emanates.

Your one-point—the phrase sounds exotic, but it has a simple and important connection to the golf setup. A breathing pattern that disturbs your stance's grounding does so above or below your one-point, the place where your upper and lower torso literally align over the ball. You need to feel a proper inhalation and exhalation through your one-point at setup. Your stance's key link to earth power depends on proper breathing.

The two breathing techniques I'm going to show you will help condition the proper cycle in your setup and swing. All you have to do is listen to your ki.

Finding Your One-Point

1. Stand with your feet shoulder-width apart, your arms at your sides (fig. 1.10a). Place your hand two inches below your navel (fig. 1.10b); this is your one-point. Leave your hand here. I suggest you tap this spot several times when you initally perform this technique; the taps "introduce" you to your one-point.

2. You will feel a slight tingling and warmth—you have activated your one-point.

3. Inhale through your nose, and you will feel a rush of air expand not only your lungs, but also your one-point (fig. 1.10c).

4. Exhale slowly through your mouth, and you will feel your one-point move inward (fig. 1.10d).

5. Breathe out completely.

6. You will feel a relaxed sensation spreading from your one-point and throughout your body, a pleasant feeling easing all stiffness from head to toe. Some students feel warmth throughout their bodies; others experience a relaxed heaviness. Both are signs of proper grounding—they have tapped into earth power.

7. Slowly and deliberately repeat the previous steps.

If you practice this technique at home, eventually you won't have to place your hand on your one-point. You can perform this breathing drill while you drive to the course, to the store, or to work; you can even do it while watching television or laying in bed.

At this point, most of my students are delighted with another benefit of ki: the sense of clarity it brings to their thoughts. As ki breathing helps ground your setup, you can focus on golf only, allowing yourself to prepare for your backswing. The relaxation that your own breathing has given your setup has also calmed the nervousness, excitement, anxiety, and frustration you

FIGURE 1.10A READY STANCE—FRONT VIEW

FIGURE 1.10B FIND THE ONE-POINT—SIDE VIEW

FIGURE 1.10C INHALE—SIDE VIEW

FIGURE 1.10D EXHALE—SIDE VIEW

carried to the tee. For a golfer at
setup, an uncluttered mind leads to
an uncluttered swing, a balanced
swing.

If you use this technique at
setup, your breathing will help
ground you in a state of perfect
relaxation. Whenever you feel two
of a flawed setup's major warning
signals—heaviness in your upper
torso and lightness in your lower
body—you can back off the ball
and, using ki breathing, restore your
connection to earth power. Then
you will be poised for the perfect
setup.

A

Visual Breathing

The next breathing technique for
your setup goes a step further than
the first. You are about to learn how
to control your inhalations and
exhalations at the critical
moment—when your setup gives
way to your backswing's motion.

1. Stand with your feet shoulder-
   width apart and with your arms
   at your sides (fig. 1.11a).
2. Begin inhaling and raise your
   arms, palms up, until your arms
   are above your head (fig. 1.11b–
   fig. 1.11e).

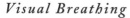

B

FIGURE 1.11 VISUAL BREATHING—FRONT VIEW
(CONTINUED ON NEXT PAGE)

C

D

F

G

E

H

3. As you inhale, expand your one-point, just as you did in the previous exercise.
4. Exhale evenly and lower your arms in front of your body, your palms facing each other (fig. 1.11f–fig. 1.11h). You will feel your one-point contract.
5. Keep repeating the whole process.

In this exercise, because you're controlling your breathing pattern and maintaining a relaxed body with your arms in motion, you're proving that you can rely on your one-point to guide you from your setup to your backswing.

SUMMARY

With your new Eastern breathing techniques, stances, and exercises, there's no reason to set up tense ever again. Practice these techniques on a regular basis:

1. The Horse
2. The Stack
3. The Swing
4. Finding your one-point
5. Visual breathing

Follow this sequence, and you will head to the course with the perfect setup and the simple keys to keep it as "solid as a mountain"—permanently. Welcome to your first lesson in Balanced Golf.

You are now ready for the next step in your journey: martial arts and your backswing. It is time for your game to experience yang.

2

THE BACKSWING—
POWER THAT FLOWS LIKE A WATERFALL

It is time to move the club and welcome the force of yang into your swing. The instant your takeaway begins, the setup's condition of yin changes into yang. The move from setup to backswing is crucial because it charts your swing's first course—and unless you get off to a smooth start, you'll have a difficult time swinging the club with balance and power.

In the previous chapter, I introduced you to the nature of yin in your setup, preparing you for its counterpart—the element of yang in your takeaway and backswing. At this stage in your swing, it's important to maintain the balance and relaxed limbs the dojo has brought to your setup. This assures you of fluid movement and the proper transfer of yang energy.

Remember the analogy we discussed in Chapter 1—water surging smoothly and powerfully through a garden hose? Let's take that image a step further. The moment the handle is turned and water flows, only a knot in the hose can slow the water's surging power. With the assistance of basic martial arts principles you can smooth out any "man-made" kinks in your backswing and unlock the consistent power flow of yang energy.

Before we head farther down the Eastern path that has led you to a solid setup, we must detour to the West and review the traditional backswing. So, it's back to the practice tee to establish a repeatable routine.

FIGURE 2.1 SETUP THROUGH BACKSWING, DRIVER—FRONT VIEW

WESTERN REVIEW— CLASSIC ELEMENTS

Knee Flex

As you move from setup to back-swing, your right knee should be flexed just as it is in your address position. Your left knee should bend inward slightly as a result of your hip and shoulder rotation. There is no set amount that the left knee should move inward. It naturally varies from player to player and must be judged on your flexibility and comfort level. However, I do caution players not to create an exaggerated motion. Why? Because your left heel will lift farther off the ground, disturbing your balance. I know what some sharp-eyed golfers will say: great players such as Jack Nicklaus and Tom Watson lift their left heel high. That's absolutely right—for them. And absolutely wrong for the average golfer. A slight lift is all it takes; this will ensure a stabilized left foot for greater balance.

Natural talent, not to mention a lifetime of practice, allows Nicklaus and Watson to stay balanced. But what works for them won't work for the amateur player. No more than

John Daly's long backswing works for the average player.

Hip Girdle

As a golf instructor has perhaps told you, the ideal rotation for your hips during the backswing is a 45-degree turn. This gives you proper weight displacement and frees up your shoulders to make a full turn.

If your hip rotation feels strained and restricted, there's a simple Western checkpoint that works well: your left-foot position. If your toes are aimed too far to the left, this will cause a limited hip-girdle rotation.

Shoulders

As you may have guessed, the ideal twisting radius for your upper body is 90 degrees. You might also know that a complete turn speeds up the swing and adds yardage—big yardage if properly executed. If you take a close look at the shoulder turns of long hitters such as John Daly, Tiger Woods, and Ernie Els, you will notice that full turn. As a matter of fact, you can probably count on one hand the number of big hitters who use a reduced shoul-der rotation.

The key to proper shoulder rotation is a basic but critical one: the relationship of your left shoulder to the ball. Simply put, your ball position programs how far your shoulder travels behind the ball in your backswing. Here's an easy way to feel what I'm talking about. Pick up one of your woods, and set up over the ball in your normal stance. Your ball is probably placed far enough forward to allow your left shoulder to navigate well behind the ball. Now, grab a mid-iron, and set up again. This time your left shoulder should be aligned slightly behind the ball. Use the following checklist as a reference guide to classic shoulder positions with different clubs:

FIGURE 2.2 TOP OF BACKSWING, DRIVER—FRONT VIEW

- Woods—left shoulder is four to six inches behind the ball (fig. 2.2).
- Long and middle irons—left shoulder is slightly (one to three inches) behind the ball (fig. 2.3).
- Short irons—left shoulder is directly in line with the ball (fig. 2.4).

FIGURE 2.3 TOP OF BACKSWING, 5-IRON—FRONT VIEW

FIGURE 2.4 TOP OF BACKSWING, PITCHING WEDGE—FRONT VIEW

Weight Distribution

Weight distribution is a critical "priming" factor in the swing. In your backswing, you must move a portion of your weight into your right side. If you don't shift your weight properly as you draw the club back, your downswing is doomed because you can't shift your weight effectively from right to left. A common flaw I see with weekend golfers is keeping too much weight on the left leg, creating a reverse pivot. This position forces you to shift your weight onto your right leg in the downswing instead of the left leg. On the flip side, if you move too much weight into your right side, it could spell disaster. Why? Because it takes quite a bit of effort to recover that much distance in your downswing.

At this point, it's important to discuss how individual clubs dictate body weight transfer and how fast each club is swung. Your short irons are, of course, your shortest clubs in length. As a result, these are the slowest swinging clubs in your bag—solely because the shaft length compels you to swing them slowly. In this case, your body weight stays relatively centered in relation to your stance during most of the swing. However, the opposite is true of your woods and long irons. Their length creates a faster swing, and therefore more body weight shifts to stabilize your balance.

Let's turn to another sport to hammer home the theory of proper weight distribution. When Greg Maddux and Roger Clemens wind up to throw a baseball, they shift most of their body weight onto their right leg. This movement resembles the same function as your shift during your backswing—loading the weight.

Upper and Lower Body Alignment

Basically, the concept of body alignments is universal and simple: the entire body must work together fluidly—as a unit. Unless your body is aligned properly for any athletic motion, whether it's a golf swing or a technique in the dojo, you will never harness maximum power, and you will never perform the motion fluidly.

FIGURE 2.5 TOP OF BACKSWING, DRIVER—SIDE VIEW

In the classic swing, your upper and lower body should be aligned directly over each other. This stacked position ensures proper weight displacement and provides a clear path for your arms to direct the club around you and into the completion of your backswing.

What happens if your alignments aren't synchronized? If your upper torso leans excessively to the left or to the right, you will surely trigger faulty impact positions and struggle for distance.

I can't stress the importance of this position enough not only for the backswing, but also for the entire swing.

TOP OF BACKSWING

Knee Flex

From a side view, your right knee tells you whether your weight displacement is working the way it should (fig. 2.5). If your knee has straightened out, you haven't transferred enough weight to your right side and have tilted your upper torso to the left. Remember that your knee bend should mimic the flex from your address position.

Waist Bend

In the backswing, you must pay close attention to the forward tilting of your waist. If you feel it moving upward or downward, you are seriously affecting your swing. Most golfers detect this problem by feeling their head rise and fall too much. However, it's the waist bend that should be blamed. Just maintain the position you established at address and you're good to go.

Right Elbow

The right elbow is a vital guide in your backswing. You must keep the separation of your elbow and torso to a minimum—if you don't, it will create a poor response in your arms and body. By being aware of the elbow position in your backswing, you will stay more connected and eliminate other possible errors.

With several students of mine, the "flying right elbow" poses a particular problem (fig. 2.6). However, it is easily fixed. Just position your right forearm more vertically to the ground and that should do the trick. Perfection is not required, but try to come as close to vertical as possible—within your own comfort level, of course.

FIGURE 2.6 TOP OF BACKSWING (FLYING RIGHT ELBOW), DRIVER—SIDE VIEW

Left Arm

In conjunction with your right elbow, your left arm can "advise" you of treacherous swing path problems. A proper backswing features a relationship between the two that you can actually feel. The length of your club governs their respective positions. As the length of the club increases, from sand wedge to driver, your left arm comes down closer and closer to the same angle as your shoulders.

Let's take a look at the driver (fig. 2.7). It has the flattest swing plane of all your clubs and should be positioned several inches above your shoulder line. Pay special attention to your left arm. What is it telling you? If your position is too low or too high, it will produce erratic impact angles for the club. Also, keep in mind that it's the shaft length that keys your left arm and shows you the perfect plane.

As you swing each consecutive club down from your driver

FIGURE 2.7 TOP OF BACKSWING, DRIVER—SIDE VIEW

(3-wood, 4-wood, 2-iron, and so on), your left arm rises in relation to your shoulder line. The nature of a shorter club, such as the sand wedge (fig. 2.8), is that you stand closer to the ball, and this in turn creates a more upright swing plane.

Clubface

Here comes one of the game's ongoing debates: is a square, open, or closed clubface position better? Guess what? In a way, the correct answer is all of the above. Each one can work for different players. The

FIGURE 2.8 TOP OF BACKSWING, SAND WEDGE—SIDE VIEW

quest is to find the one that feels most comfortable and produces the most consistent results.

We need to put on the brakes for a moment and look at all three positions:

- Square—the clubface is angled with your shoulder line (fig. 2.9).
- Open—the toe of your club is aimed directly at the ground (fig. 2.10).
- Closed—the entire clubface is pointing up at the sky (fig. 2.11).

I have to admit that I'm a purist when it comes to clubface angle. I advocate a square position, and I do so for good reason: a square clubface allows you to hit a wider range of shots. In case you're wondering, I practice what I preach—I use the square approach.

If you opt for the open or closed position, you must realize that the clubface works in opposites. By that, I mean that if your clubface is open on the backswing, you will close it in the downswing. If your clubface is closed in the backswing, you will open it in the downswing. It's simple physics and it has a deep effect

FIGURE 2.9 TOP OF BACKSWING (SQUARE CLUB-FACE), DRIVER—SIDE VIEW

FIGURE 2.10 TOP OF BACKSWING (OPEN CLUB-FACE), DRIVER—SIDE VIEW

FIGURE 2.11 TOP OF BACKSWING (CLOSED CLUB-FACE), DRIVER—SIDE VIEW

the natural talent of these two great players.

Shaft Alignment

For the moment, I just want you to focus on one key reference concerning your club shaft alignment in the backswing: at the top of your backswing, the shaft should be parallel to the target line. If it is aimed to the left or right, it will redirect the path of your club and cause very erratic shot patterns.

I will wait until the next chapter on the transition to discuss how faulty shaft alignments harm the performance of your swing.

on your shots, especially when using a closed-to-open angle. This technique is tough to master because, even in the hands of a good player, the clubface angle tends to create heavy, or fat, shots. Remember, if the clubface is closed the leading edge is much lower than the back edge and this makes you "shovel" the ball. Although Lee Trevino and Paul Azinger play brilliantly with the closed-to-open position, I guide most students away from it, teaching the virtues of a square face because most players don't possess

BACK TO THE EAST

Now, let's put the clubs back in the bag, and return to the dojo to learn more about natural law and its importance to a fluid backswing. Pay attention to the details in each of the following principles, because they give you the foundation that marries your Western and Eastern Balanced Golf swing.

Yin and Yang Body Motion

Once again, we turn to the principle of yin and yang. The reason for applying this theory to your back-swing is to create a smooth transition from the yin state of your setup to the movement of your club, or the yang state. If you can feel and control this exchange of motion, you will maintain a balanced foundation throughout your backswing.

The two most important points of consideration should be:

- There is no sudden change of motion when the backswing begins.
- Your grip pressure does not substantially increase.

If you violate either of these two factors, you violate the proper function of yin and yang.

In the dojo, if you cannot effectively and smoothly yield from yin to yang, you are in deep trouble. Your training partner will find this weakness and use it against you. Remember that whenever you are moving, your body is constantly changing yin and yang forces. The sharp-eyed martial artist is always trying to take advantage of this natural law and defeat his or her opponent. Don't let yourself be defeated.

Posture and Balance

You have the Eastern tools to set up solid as a mountain from the elements we discussed in Chapter 1—the Horse and the Stack. Now that you have a great setup, you must maintain it in the backswing to get optimal results. Your base is the foundation to control the upcoming weight transfer and give you the stability for proper body mechanics. Because we have anchored your setup's balance, you possess a terrific swing key—you are programmed with an innate ability to control weight transfer. "How?" you might ask. Well, there is a rule in natural law that uncovers this truth; it's called *strength of stance*. This law teaches us that we can control lateral motion in the backswing solely based on lower body positioning. The Horse stance (or, in our case, the golf stance) has the strongest line of resistance from side to side, and this represents—you've got it—lateral motion.

The next crucial question is, how much weight transfer is correct? There is a simple yet varied answer. Keep in mind that your driver is the longest and fastest swinging club and that your wedges are the shortest and slowest moving clubs. For this reason, more weight is transferred with your driver than with your wedges. The following guidelines will help you figure out how much weight to transfer into your right side:

Driver—85 percent
Fairway woods—75 percent
Long irons—70 percent
Middle irons—65 percent
Short irons—60 percent

To continue, if you have a sound posture and good balance throughout the backswing, you greatly increase your chances of success. However, if you alter a position in your posture, you will adversely affect the path of your club and hit poor shots.

The dojo provides any number of drastic examples of what happens to effective motion if one's "tower of balance" crumbles. An error that seems minor—a straightening of the knees, an increase in waist bend—can ruin posture. On the mat, I often illustrate this point by having a student take the offensive against me by striking with a right-handed punch and stepping forward (fig. 2.12a). I

counter with a wedging technique that deflects his strike and knocks him off balance (fig. 2.12b–fig. 2.12c). From there, his balance is broken and any follow-up technique will have severely reduced power.

From a golfing standpoint, the lesson is that if your posture is troubled, you lose serious control and power in your swing. How do you maintain your posture as you actually begin to swing the club? By keeping your upper torso and lower body stacked. You must keep them over one another. A classic example of perfectly stacked body alignments is Ernie Els. Next time you're watching him on TV, or if you're lucky enough to see him in person at a tournament, study his stacking position. He turns into his backswing without altering his posture, winding and coiling for the soon-to-follow explosive power in his downswing. Without such proper attributes, there would be no 300-yard drives. Study this!

Joint Rounding

We are back to rounded joints, your best defense against the Western swing's worst enemy—rigidity. Earlier we discussed what rigid

A

B

C

FIGURE 2.12 WEDGING—SIDE VIEW

limbs can do to the golf swing, how they can destroy the smooth exchange of yin and yang. Now, however, I'm going to reveal how to carry "looseness," or fluidity, into your takeaway and backswing.

Once the motion of your club begins in the backswing, your arms must stay relaxed. The left arm doesn't hyperextend, nor does the right arm stay straight. They both move in a relaxed yet extended fashion. Remember, the left arm controls the width (arc) of your swing, so it must be extended, just not rigid. There is a happy medium somewhere, and it's up to you to find your own comfort level. Your arms should feel taut—not too soft, not too hard.

Also, you must allow your right arm to fold naturally so that the upper portion (the humerus) can maintain reasonable contact with your torso during most of the back-swing. Again, not to sound too redundant, if your right arm stays extended and rigid, it will affect how the club moves around your body.

In the dojo, I demonstrate the value of joint rounding in numerous ways, one of which is the Unbend-able Arm. This is a combination of mental focus and relaxation. I begin by relaxing my body, making all the joints soft and rounded. With my arm extended, I let my students try to bend it with all the force they can generate (fig. 2.13). Do you think they can? The answer is a definite no! You see, I project my mental focus and imagine that my arm is like a firehose shooting out power-ful water that nothing can stop. That image and my relaxed joints are an unstoppable combination. However, if I were to tense up and straighten out my arm, it would be quite easy for my students to col-lapse it. It's hard to believe, but you

FIGURE 2.13 UNBENDABLE ARM—SIDE VIEW

are actually weaker when you harden up your body. Try this experiment for yourself.

Exercises

To help you develop the attributes we just discussed, I have included two exercises that complement and apply their usage. They are simplis-tic in nature, but they hit the nail right on the head when it comes to the actual function of your golf swing.

Body Rotation I

1. Start in a wide Horse stance, flexing your knees (fig. 2.14a).

2. Lift your arms, positioning the right arm vertically and the left arm horizontally (fig. 2.14a). Keep both hands open, forming a V with your right thumb and index finger. An easy way to accomplish this is to think of your hand position as an aiming sight on a rifle.

3. Turn in both directions as far as you can without feeling strain, keeping your arms extended but relaxed (fig. 2.14b–fig. 2.14h). Because the motion in your hips is restricted, your upper body will feel obstructed as well. This makes turning completely to the left and right somewhat difficult. That's normal. Just remember, you should only be twisting as far as your comfort level allows. Also, the cadence from side to side is slow. Don't try moving too quickly, as that only makes your muscles tighten. You should be relaxed the whole time. When you see a marksman at work, his entire body and the rifle move as one unit whenever he turns to shoot another target.

FIGURE 2.14 BODY ROTATION I—FRONT VIEW

A golfer's body, head, and club should move in this same type of unison.

Okay, you have performed the exercise a few times. Now you're wondering what it's doing for your backswing. If you've kept your arms loose, turning from side to side, you're developing the relaxed synchronized power that world-class players use. Pretty soon, you will be able to feel this unity of arm and body motion constantly. The freedom of tension in your arms is incredible and if you ever sense any sudden tightening in them, stop, and start this exercise again. I highly suggest that if you feel rigid, you reestablish your one-point through our breathing techniques from Chapter 1. Then, repeat the movements of Body Rotation I. You will soon experience that winning combination of fluid and relaxed movement.

As you turn in both directions with your arms extended, the motion might initially seem mechanical, or even robotic. Believe it or not, this is a desired Eastern element for the golf swing. The trick is to recognize both in your mind and in your body that just because proper rotation requires the same alignments every time, this motion is not mechanically stiff. In other words, your body performs the same movements smoothly and repetitively. Your arm and body motions mold into one solid, synchronized piece. When turning in both directions, you'll feel a pure, unforced connection between your arms and body rotation. In the dojo, this translates into precise and fluid techniques. On the golf course, a "one-piece" rotation translates into a smooth, powerful swing.

In perhaps its greatest gift to the golf swing, Body Rotation I brings another element of natural law to your game by freeing up your entire body—not just your arms—to unleash the power of yang in your backswing. The more you practice this exercise, the more you'll grasp its truth: your arms are just coming along for the ride, and even as you transfer weight in the backswing, your entire body is doing the work, not just your arms.

Before you learn Body Rotation II, which is your next step on the Eastern path to Balanced Golf, let's quickly review what Body Rotation I does:

• Relaxes your arms
• Rounds out your upper back

- Develops a smooth cadence, helping the start of your back-swing
- Connects your arms and body into one fluidly turning machine
- Allows your upper body—not just your arms—to do the work

It is important to note that you can't listen to the adage "no pain, no gain." If you feel any discomfort, never mind pain, when you move beyond a certain point, stop immediately. Listen to your body. As your flexibility improves—which it can through the techniques and exercises of Balanced Golf—your range of comfortable motion also will increase. Again, if you experience a twinge or some strain, stop. Turn only as far as you comfortably can.

You now hold the first key to a balanced, repeatable backswing in a perfect blend of East and West. Now, it's time to expand what you've learned in Body Rotation I. How can you do this? Just follow along and you'll see what I mean as Body Rotation II guides your way.

Body Rotation II

This exercise is more complex than Body Rotation I, but don't worry—complex is a relative term. Body Rotation II is not a difficult discipline of the dojo. But this exercise is a key one for the golfer, a building block for a balanced swing from backswing to finish. "What is the mystery in Body Rotation II?" you ask. There is no Chinese riddle here—just simple, solid Eastern principles that mirror a fluid golf swing and only require that you practice them.

In one essential way, Body Rotation II is much different than any other dojo technique you've learned so far. In performing this new exercise, you can use a club. If we were in my dojo, I would hand you a three-foot-long martial arts staff called a *jo*. But there's no need for you to go shopping at a martial arts academy. You already have what you need in your golf bag—a 6-iron. Your club is a perfect substitute for the jo.

Now that you're properly equipped with your 6-iron for Body Rotation II, let's get started on this balanced blend of golf and the martial arts:

1. Assume your normal setup stance—your feet shoulder width apart, your knees flexed, and your body bent slightly forward from the waist.

2. Grasp the jo (your 6-iron) with your right hand, palm facing upward, and your left hand, palm facing downward. Make sure your hands are about 10 inches apart. Hold the jo out in front of you with your arms extended (fig. 2.15a).

   Picture yourself on the course. Guess what? The jo, or 6-iron, is positioned parallel to the target line. You are already off to a great start with the exercise.

3. Swing the jo to the right as you normally do in your backswing, but only move it three-quarters of the way back (fig. 2.15b–fig. 2.15c). If you try to make a full backswing with your hands 10 inches apart, it will disrupt the posture and balance you've already achieved.

   There's something else you have to do as you swing the jo—watch the ball. Because this exercise simulates your golf swing, it's important to make eye contact with your normal ball position.

   Also, as you draw the jo back, you might feel your left heel raise slightly—and that's okay! Actually, a slight lift with your heel proves that weight has shifted to your right side, just as it should in your golf swing.

4. After completing your three-quarter backswing, begin swinging the jo to the left and into your downswing (fig. 2.15d).

5. Continue the motion until you move into a normal finish position (fig. 2.15e–fig. 2.15f). A word of caution here: at the finish, you want your arms extended out in front of you and not up into a high finish (fig. 2.15f).

I have instructed you to perform steps 4 and 5 even though they go beyond the backswing motion. I will be discussing these elements in much greater depth in the following chapters, for both are crucial elements to your Eastern-style transition, downswing, impact, and follow-through. But I want you to feel Body Rotation II's most important applications to natural law—

A

B

C

D

E

F

FIGURE 2.15 BODY ROTATION II—FRONT VIEW

body alignments and lateral motion—from your backswing to your finish. If I ask you to stop the jo at the end of the three-quarter backswing, it will break the connection, the flow—and we can't let this happen. It is vital to allow the jo and its golf-swing–simulating movements to develop unification of your body and arms from the takeaway to the finish.

There is another reason I want you to swing the jo from takeaway to finish. Body Rotation II compels you to shift your weight and that's another step up the ladder to a balanced golf swing.

Again, as you practice Body Rotation II, you'll soon feel how your body, your arms, and, to a lesser degree, your head work in unison. And, while the 10 inches between your hands on the jo or 6-iron will take some getting used to at first, you'll feel the combination of the jo and your body move in a synchronized fashion through the takeaway and backswing.

As with the Horse and your breathing patterns, you can use both body rotation exercises not only at home, but also on the course. If something doesn't feel quite right

with your backswing on the first hole or two, turn to these two exercises. The hidden beauty of both is that they look like you're just limbering up—not performing time-tested techniques of the dojo. But you'll know the truth. You will know that your head, arms, and body are working together—connected. How will you know? Repetition of the body rotation exercises will tell you. Follow them, and you'll reach the transition from backswing to downswing with your body stacked, your joints rounded, and your posture a tower of balance. These Eastern steps add up to a repeatable Western backswing every time you begin your takeaway.

Summary

At this point in our journey, I would like you to review all the material we've covered so far and make sure you have a firm hold on the routines of the Western setup and backswing. Then, study the Eastern techniques that have given you the tools to balance those two components every time. I know, you're asking why I want you to do the same homework twice. My answer is that our next step—the transition—is so important to the Balanced Golf marriage of East and West that you must be completely comfortable with the Horse, the Stack, Body Rotations I and II, and every other technique and principle we've discussed so far. I promise you that if you focus and refocus on how far you've already come, you'll master this Eastern approach and be prepared for the moment of truth in your downswing. You will also be amazed at the gifts yin and yang are about to bring to you. And these gifts will truly last for the life of your game.

3

THE TRANSITION—
THE ZONE OF FLUIDITY

We are now heading into one of the most dangerous parts of your swing—the transition. This major event lies in the function of your downswing and is a deciding factor to the overall success of any swing you make. Keep in mind that if a problem rears its head during this time span, you'll hit only a mediocre shot at best.

To isolate the characteristics of your transition, allow me to specify its features. The moment your backswing ends and the club changes direction to start downward, you are in your transition. This moment is significant because whenever you change the direction of a physical motion, an error can occur. To take it one step further and tie in the principle of yin and yang, you need to pay attention here. The yang energy that has guided your club in the backswing must now yield at the top, or ending, of your backswing.

This momentary pause creates a yin state and allows the club to move down into impact very fluidly. By executing this sequence properly, you'll be rewarded with grand results. The finished product will be a crisp, solid shot. And I'm sure you won't argue with that outcome!

Once you make it through the land mines of your transition, you will be moving perfectly into the impact area. As might be expected, there are numerous model positions you're trying to achieve at impact, and in the following chapter I will explain them in detail.

WESTERN TRANSITION TIME

Let's head back to the practice tee for the next Western lesson, the classic but hard-to-master transition zone.

A

B

C

D

FIGURE 3.1 THE END OF THE BACKSWING AND BEGINNING OF THE DOWNSWING, DRIVER—FRONT VIEW

Left Arm and Lag

Once you are into your transition, a key element to additional power is the lag. The *lag* can be defined as the stored explosive power your wrists contribute during the downswing. To give you a Kodak moment, it's the angle your left arm and club shaft create in the transition and downswing—which, by the way, should be around a 90-degree angle. If you can retain this position during the start of your downswing, you will add a considerable amount of yardage to any club in your bag.

However, it's not uncommon for golfers to prerelease their wrists in the transition stage. This is a natural tendency, but one that should be avoided at all costs. Most players fall prey to this mistake by twisting their body too much and/or keeping too much weight on their right leg when the downswing begins. That's a big mistake. As you'll see in the 1-2-3 Count exercise later in this chapter, the transition is led by the body. If you can start your downswing by nudging your body to the left, it will assist you with the lag.

The last key here is to allow your arms to drop downward when you start the downswing. By doing so, you'll increase your chances of maintaining the proper wrist angle and allowing this power source to follow its combustible nature. Occasionally, I give my students the mental image of chopping wood—the axe is obviously substituted for your club. Suggesting a picture of the arm dropping downward to the right hip, instead of swinging out away from the body, definitely helps with their perception of this concept.

Left Heel

For a fluid transition and downswing, your left heel must be firmly planted on the ground. This sounds easy, but it seems like I've had more students than I can count—some of them competent players—whose heels move and throw them off balance. Sometimes it's subtle, barely enough to notice; other times, it's impossible to miss. But no matter how much lift there is, it's a problem.

Your balance structure will be fragmented if you raise your heel during the transition. By doing so, you're simply opening the door of opportunity for other mechanical problems in your swing. And I have to believe that you're not eager for that situation.

Remember, you gain power from the ground up, and without solid footwork, you're robbing yourself of this valuable resource.

Knees

As you move from the top of your backswing through your downswing, the space between your knees should not decrease. If anything, it will widen a little. This will ensure sound balance and keep your lower body from rotating too rapidly. Generally speaking, players who are very fast in the transition tend to fire the right knee inward and change the spacing in their lower body. This causes a timing problem with the upper and lower body alignments—not to mention sending the club into a panic attack mode, creating every imaginable shot.

I think the lower body positioning of Sam Snead is a classic example. Mr. Snead is acknowledged as one of the greatest technicians the game has ever known and is highly regarded by his peers for many accomplishments. Among the many physical techniques he refined, his lower body control was second to none. He moved through the transition of his swing with what appeared to be a slight squatting motion. His knees actually looked like they were spreading farther apart. The by-product of this type of control is that the twisting motion is slowed and more power is stored for impact.

Keep in mind that it's the straightening of your knees that directly affects when and how much your lower body turns. So, maintain a flexed position and keep that space open.

Upper and Lower Body Alignments

For a balanced transition and downswing, your upper torso and lower body must be aligned with one another. I liken this position to the skewer that a chef would use to cook meats and vegetables. This is what you need to visualize as the tool that holds your alignment together from head to toe. For the golfer, all your body parts will maintain correct positioning and move together if properly aligned. No part should ever move without the others—this creates a unison of motion and allows all body parts to work together as a unit.

There are, however, many golfers who violate the arrangement of this body posture. Some lead the downswing with just their lower body, while others tilt their upper bodies to the left. In either case, some terrible results will surface.

By now, you can probably guess that I'm a big believer in large parts controlling the swing. One of those large parts is the use of your body in its entirety, and that means it must stay aligned. One of the best images you can rely on is the skewer theory I've already mentioned. With some practice, you should be able to visualize this object running down your spine and apply the concept as needed. Once you can do this on autopilot, you won't have to strain for longer, straighter shots.

THE EASTERN PATH

The steps in the previous section are the classic Western transition elements. It's time to move back to the dojo so that we can explore the simple steps for building a complete and repeatable transition on your journey to Balanced Golf.

Yin and Yang Body Motion

Earlier, I told you that your arms are along for the ride, working in unison with all of your body in the golf swing. The principle of yin and yang is going to be present during all of these physical motions because natural law mandates this type of action. However, it's up to the golfer to develop a fluid exchange of energy and maximize its truest potential. Nowhere in your swing are these forces more important than in the transition from backswing to downswing. You cannot strike the ball cleanly if the flow of yin and yang is disrupted at any time during the transition. This energy exchange must be unforced and natural. No strain, no fuss, just a simple change of direction.

In my dojo, any transition in movement determines the effectiveness of techniques ranging from kicks and hand maneuvers to the application of theories to real-life conditions. All of these motions, no matter how simple or complex, share a common connection: a relaxed exchange of yin and yang at the moment of transition. If, at transition, a martial artist is rigid or off balance in any way, any follow-up motion will be weakened at best, ruined at worst. Loss of power during the technique is guaranteed. The same scenario is sadly true for a golfer whose posture and arm motions are not synchronized for the relaxed exchange of yin and yang.

The golfer's key to understanding the momentary yin condition that presents itself at the top of the backswing and then changes into the yang state of the downswing is one basic fact: you are switching the direction of your swing. This is a critical moment because any change, any shift in athletic motion, demands a smooth and consistent flow of yin and yang energy.

I find it useful to picture yin and yang as an electric current. You need to maintain a strong and steady surge of energy in your golf swing from setup to finish. However, if you suddenly disrupt that flow by decreasing or increasing the speed of your downswing, you have broken your swing's current. A "brownout"—slowing of your downswing—will cause your arms and club to lag behind the twisting motion of your body. Conversely, a swing "surge"—a sudden increase in your downswing's tempo—will push your arms and club way ahead of your body. Even if you make what seems like solid contact, it's an illusion! You are unbalanced and soon enough the odds will catch up to you, stealing distance and direction.

For a martial artist, such misalignments during transitions can be a painful disaster. For instance, someone who is transitioning poorly as he or she comes at me on the mat will be subdued and have no other recourse of action. On the course, a golfer who has disrupted the flow of transition simply can't counter the mistake before impact. Sure, he or she may still get a piece of the ball, but the shot won't be anywhere as solid or as long as it should be. When I have a student with an aggressive swing who counters this point with a comment such as "yes, but I drove it 250 yards even though I sped up my downswing," I can quickly answer, "but you'll hit more fairways and still launch those long tee shots if you just keep the principle of yin and yang working in your corner." That gets attention!

This is why the transition, the connection between backswing and downswing, is so essential, every bit as much as a martial artist's transition from a ready stance to an explosive kick or hand technique. This is also why we have to talk a little more about the concept of yin and yang in your transition and downswing.

For all but the most gifted golfers, speed kills—either too much or too little. As I've told hundreds of students, it destroys consistent and repeatable rhythm and flow—the very ingredients you need for a balanced Western swing. Several of the Eastern principles and techniques I have already established in your game can take you several steps further on the path to Balanced Golf. However, with a few new insights from the martial arts' vault of knowledge, you can produce solid shots with every club in your bag.

At this point, you're probably saying, "I understand yin and yang, but I've always had trouble maintaining the same speed in two different directions, backswing and downswing." Although you don't yet realize it, you have a solution already—music. I know, this may sound like it has no relation to your swing, but bear with me. I think you will see the connection between composers, martial artists, and golfers.

To me, the yin and yang of a balanced swing or a crisp martial arts technique definitely mimics the cadence of classical music. How can this be? The notes play smoothly in the hands of skilled musicians; nothing breaks the flow—the current—of that music. That is what you're aiming for in the golf swing. You want to compose a smooth surge of body, mind, and club or, for the martial artist, of body and mind. This is the ultimate goal and achievable for anyone who has the gumption to give it a try. Go ahead and take a portable stereo or Walkman the next time you go out to the practice tee. Listen to your favorite musician and follow the rhythm of the songs—you'll be amazed how the flow helps your swing pace. I would encourage you to select songs without lyrics, though. It's just much easier to hear the cadence of instrumental pieces.

Often, when I've stood by such classic shotmakers as Larry Mize or Steve Elkington, the comparison of golf and music really comes to mind. They are so rhythmic in nature that their transitions just flow like a concerto, giving them exceptional results. They carry the same tempo before and after the transition. It is similar to the way music flows smoothly from one bar of notes to the next. This is what simple martial arts principles can bring to your game. They will give you the keys, the "notes," for the even flow of energy as you change the direction of your swing.

Joint Rounding

Although you have reached the top of your backswing with rounded joints and you are primed to keep them supple in the downswing, one of them can still defeat you—if you let it. It's your left elbow.

In the dojo, my students learn that locking an elbow immediately puts them in a precarious position for counters, not to mention little hope for additional techniques. A slight bend in the elbow is essential. If it's not there, stiffness will spread from the elbow into the entire body and disrupt power output. Remember, if you lock your arm, you've used up 100 percent of your energy—and any skilled martial artist knows that you must have energy in reserve. By not over-extending your arm, you will keep an extra supply of energy so that your balance structure isn't heavily taxed. This is precisely why joint rounding is an effective way for releasing power while maintaining sound swing mechanics.

Now, you're wondering again how this principle of the training

hall translates to the golf course. You probably have an even bigger question about the left elbow: how can I talk about a bent elbow in the golf swing when traditional Western swing teachers command you to keep your left arm straight at the top of the backswing? This is where I need you to pay special attention to the Eastern concept of joint rounding. Despite the traditional Western commandment to keep your left arm locked, you can bend your elbow a little. In fact, a slight elbow bend in your transition is not only desirable, but natural. How do I know this? From many years of experience and research on the mat and on the course. I'm going to show you how a slight amount of elbow bend sculpted to you and your own physical traits is a subtle yet strategic building block for a smooth and balanced downswing.

Here's why proper joint rounding is so crucial to your transition and downswing. As you poise your club at the top of the backswing, a force of nature that neither a golfer nor a martial artist can defy comes into play—it's *centrifugal force*. You might remember its characteristics from a physics course. Basically, it is the outward pulling force that is generated from the twisting motion of your body.

Centrifugal force will elongate your elbow and extend your left arm as you take your downswing. You can't do anything about this. Whether you like it or not, centrifugal force carries you to impact, and you have to learn not to fight this law. As a matter of fact, martial artists welcome centrifugal force. It allows us to blend with an opponent so that powerful techniques and throws can be used. Golfers, too, must learn to accept this tugging force as a friend, not a foe.

The best way for golfers to work with centrifugal force is through joint rounding. If your limbs—particularly the left elbow at transition and downswing—are rounded, centrifugal force, or yang, will pull you fluidly into impact. If your elbow is too stiff and if your left arm is not only too straight, but rigid, your entire body and swing will similarly stiffen. The tower of balance and body alignments you've worked so hard to build will be shattered. On the mat, a foe would discipline you for such breakdowns; on the course, your punishment is loss of power and joint stress—along with the emotional strain that spoils a round.

In your setup, the Horse, the Stack, and correct posture have helped round out your joints. You have felt how Body Rotations I and II require your upper torso, your lower body, and your limbs to work in fluid unison. Now, however, as your backswing reaches its top position, you will lose everything you've gained if you straighten your left arm and elbow so much that they're rigid. Again, I'll emphasize an iron-clad rule in martial arts training: rigidity is the ultimate enemy of fluid movement. It is certainly the ultimate enemy of your transition and downswing.

So how much elbow bend is the right amount? Of course, I don't want you to think I'm suggesting that you loosen your elbow so much that your left arm is waving around. This would ruin your swing's balance every bit as much as a severe lockup of the joint. Instead, I advocate what we began with at setup: a relaxed and slightly bent left elbow. As golfers travel from takeaway to transition, their personal physical attributes, as well as limitations, really come into play. Everyone's elbow must straighten, but for most players, at any level, a slight elbow bend is natural and allows them to move smoothly from transition to the centrifugal force of the downswing.

Still wondering how much bend is allowable for Balanced Golf? Here's a case where a picture—or two—is truly worth a thousand words (fig. 3.2–fig. 3.5).

Through my teaching on the tee and in the training hall, I've discovered that the elbow position shown in Figure 3.4 is a comfortable yet minimal bend that allows most players to maintain the qualities of acceptable joint rounding. This subtle bend in the elbow is good for

FIGURE 3.2 SETUP (RELAXED LEFT ARM), 6-IRON—FRONT VIEW

FIGURE 3.3 SETUP (RIGID LEFT ARM), 6-IRON—FRONT VIEW

FIGURE 3.4 TOP OF BACKSWING (RELAXED LEFT ARM), 6-IRON—FRONT VIEW

FIGURE 3.5 TOP OF BACKSWING (RIGID LEFT ARM), 6-IRON—FRONT VIEW

anyone who is so conscious of keeping the left arm straight that rigidity creeps up and into the transition, producing a questionable downswing. I have embraced this slight bend in my own swing, and if you want further PGA-style proof, take a good look at Freddie Couples, Curtis Strange, and Lee Janzen. You will find that they all bend the elbow slightly.

There are, of course, great swingers such as Greg Norman who use extended left arm positions. When I have had a student present this type of motion and it's not impeding any other portion of the swing, I leave him or her alone! However, I do strongly encourage most players to unlock the elbow just a little bit. My advice? Don't be afraid to bend!

Strength of Stance

We are back to the Horse—that's right, your Eastern golf stance. It's one of those techniques that is so much more than it appears at first look. It has a lot to contribute in your transition and downswing. The Horse will lead you to the key position of your downswing—lateral motion.

The strength of the Horse/golf stance is how it anchors or grounds you for side-to-side movement, allowing you to control weight transfer in your swing. With the help of the Horse and our other Eastern guides, you have already shifted your weight properly in the backswing; the strength of your stance, thanks to the Horse, has let you control the weight shift to your right side. Now, with the stability this stance provides, you can also control weight transfer to the left, which occurs with your downswing. As with your backswing, the Horse helps lay the foundation for your weight transfer and the lateral force of the downswing. This simple yet sophisticated stance engineers your continuing acceptance of that force.

To illustrate just how important a stable, well-measured stance is to the downswing, let's detour for a moment from the dojo to the tee and take a closer look at a PGA Tour player who has probably left you, like me, awed by his talent. Among his peers, he acquired the nickname of the "Launching Pad" because of his long drives. I'm talking about Davis Love III, and certainly one of the trademarks of his lengthy tee shots was a long backswing and follow-through. From time to time, Davis used to struggle with his accuracy off the tee. He eventually realized that his excessive swinging motion not only catapulted drives a long way, but also contributed to those straying shots. Some great players are so stubborn that they refuse to make adjustments in their game, but Davis was willing to make a change, to sacrifice some distance for more control and stability. He had the courage to identify a problem and opted for a smoother, more compact swing. In the end, this meant that his transition was destined to be more consistent than

ever before—and he's gone on to be one of the must successful players in the '90s.

How did he correct the problem? Take a look at him during televised tournaments and you will see the answer. As a matter of fact, take a look at him, and think about the Horse stance he uses. His foundation, his posture, mirrors that of our simple but powerful Eastern guide, that very same Horse. You will notice that Davis's lower body is grounded, making the rest of his swing mechanics flow quite easily. But without the principle of strength of stances working for you as it does for Davis, you can't maximize your effectiveness with side-to-side motion during the transition.

I am not about to suggest that everyone can achieve Davis's results. His talent and his dedication are unique. But you, too, can ensure that your lower body is correctly spaced for a fluid, manageable transition and downswing. If you rely on the Horse, it will show you the proper way to transfer body weight. And because you've become acquainted with this Eastern guide, you can make an adjustment in your stance and move with the refined motion of world-class players.

Finding the correct width to your stance may take a little trial and error, but once you find your comfort zone, your transition and downswing will take on a whole new feeling. The solid and connective impressions you will have in your lower body will make you feel like you can shoot a cannon into your downswing. If you just follow your instincts, the Horse will show you the proper spacing for your personal stance. How will you know? You'll know because your arms will be along for the downswing's ride in total synchronization with your stacked torso, your smooth weight transfer, and your fluid rotation. What will this feel like? When you are changing the direction of your swing, you'll feel almost nothing at all. That's how smooth a balanced transition and downswing, with the Horse's help, can be.

The 1-2-3 Count

Now I want to introduce you to a key exercise for developing the ultimate transition with all of your clubs. Whenever I describe the ideal sequencing in a golf swing to one of my students, I invariably talk about the 1-2-3 Count. This numbering system gives any golfer a clear focus on how the swing should be synchronized.

1. The 1 count represents your backswing. This includes the turning motion of your body and arms, along with the appropriate amount of weight shift onto your right leg.
2. The 2 count represents the start of your downswing—the transition. For this exercise, I have the student strictly focus on how the body leads the downswing.
3. The 3 count represents how and when your arms are incorporated into the downswing.

Now that you are aware of the proper timing, let me explain further. I usually have a student grab a 6-iron and follow along with me as I repeat the 1-2-3 Count over and over. If you start in your normal setup position and swing the club into your backswing, that's your number 1 count (fig. 3.6a–fig.3.6d). You should have a fluid start and use both your arms and body in the twisting motion of the club's going back. In addition, there should be a slight loading of weight on your right side—that's your lateral motion.

FIGURE 3.6 S ETUP INTO BACKSWING, 6-IRON—FRONT VIEW

Here's where it gets ticklish; when you start the downswing—your transition—you must move your body first (fig. 3.7a–fig. 3.7b). This represents the 2 count. What most golfers do, however, doesn't resemble this at all. They start the transition with a twisting motion of the body, and/or they move the arms first. This is the worst possible choice you can make in your downswing. If your transition begins with either of these two mistakes, you may as well mark down a bogey or worse on your scorecard. I have to emphasize again that your downswing must begin with your body. What I'm really talking about is a slight lateral motion to your left. There are many, many reasons why you must strive to repeat this pattern but the two most important are the following:

• Your lateral motion delays the twisting motion of your body, which in turn stores more power

A   B

FIGURE 3.7 DOWNSWING, 6-IRON—FRONT VIEW

for you to take into the impact area, giving you longer shots with much more consistency.

• Your arms will follow a downward path, creating a slotlike effect that will guarantee solid impact. It is hard to believe that just a simple bump of your body into the left side will pave such a superhighway for your arms to follow, but it's true.

Once the 2 count has been initiated correctly, you then allow your arms to swing down and follow through into your normal finish (fig. 3.8a–fig. 3.8f). That's your 3 count. This count may seem like the easiest, but it's always the culprit when a problem emerges. All too often I see golfers trying to hit the ball using the strength and speed of their arms. When this happens, the 2 count is substituted with the arms, which you know, should really be the 3 count. If you fall into this category don't fret—it's a common problem. You will gain peace of mind by practicing the 1-2-3 Count and developing the synchronized elements of a great swing.

Let me add one other bit of insight at this time. If you watch any world-class players —Greg Norman, Ernie Els, Nick Price, or Nick Faldo—they time the second

A

D

B

C

E

F

FIGURE 3.8 DOWNSWING INTO FINISH, 6-IRON—FRONT VIEW

and third beats of this exercise together. "Now wait a minute," you're probably saying. "If that's the way great PGA Tour players do it, why can't I duplicate their action?" Well, there's an important reason why. They have honed their swings by hitting countless golf balls, most of them under the watchful eye of a fine instructor. As a result, these players have brilliant swing mechanics and can produce those results on a consistent basis. I don't know how many average golfers can say that. For that reason, it is critical for players with transition problems to practice the 1-2-3 Count just as I've laid it out. Then, maybe one day, you can advance your skill high enough to do both the second and third counts together. I think setting a goal to be proficient in this department is a vital one and should be undertaken by any serious golfer.

Lastly, when you begin practicing this method, it is important to do it with a very staccato count. That way, you make each segment defined and clearly felt. If they are all jumbled together, you just can't focus on any one particular component. Once you can do this repetitively, you'll then have the ability to self-command the timing sequence in your swing. By breaking each count out separately, your skill will develop quickly. Pretty soon you will be hitting long shots with this pattern automatically and repeatedly. I promise you better results if you're dedicated to this system of refining your swing sequence. Train hard!

SUMMARY

You have taken a giant step in this chapter. You have discovered the Eastern tools to change the direction of your Western swing without the loss of rhythm, speed, or power. The flow of energy in your downswing is carrying it to Balanced Golf's next milestone, impact—your swing's ultimate yang.

4

IMPACT—

THE MOMENT OF TRUTH

You are at impact, the moment we've been pursuing since you greeted the Horse in your setup and welcomed the jo into your backswing and downswing. This is where East and West meet the ball—impact, the moment of truth for any golfer of any skill level.

In the previous chapters, I revealed simple martial arts principles and exercises that united your body, arms, and club for a smooth exchange of yin and yang from the setup through the downswing:

Setup—Yin
Takeaway and Backswing—
   Yang
Transition—Yin
Downswing—Yang

Now, as impact approaches and yang energy guides your clubhead to its target, your swing is triggered with balance and power. And it's all because you've embraced the Eastern keys of a classic swing. You are right on target for the best-balanced swing of your life if. . . . That's right, another "if." But this is a big one. If you do anything—I repeat, anything—to alter your yang energy this deep into the downswing, everything will fall apart. You must not short-circuit this smooth and dynamic guidance system at the very moment it's about to send the ball for a ride.

It's not that you or any golfer consciously wants to cut the flow of yang at impact. But swing malfunctions in this area are one of the biggest challenges that any golf instructor faces. Believe me, I know this. In my many years as a teaching professional, I have encountered a lot of players who did just about everything right until impact. As a matter of fact, when my teaching method unfolded from many years of serious training, I began to realize that the answers to curing pupils' poor impact lay not only in the classic foundation of the Western swing, but also in another place, where nothing is more important than fluid motion and powerful impact. You've probably guessed where I'm headed here—the dojo.

I can assure you from the bumps and bruises I earned on my way to black belt status that in the dojo, faulty impact, from failure to maintain balance and to control yang energy, hurts. Unbalanced strikes and parries not only allow an opponent to take advantage of you on the mat, but can cause joint stress and muscle pulls even in well-conditioned martial arts students. I also have to say that faulty impact for the golfer sparks its own "hurt." It comes in several painful varieties: shanks, hooks, slices, and so on. You have probably known people who couldn't seem to hit the ball cleanly and consistently no matter how hard they tried, and tossed their clubs into the basement or the garage—for good. Well, that's certainly unnecessary, because there are clear-cut ways to fix poor impact positions in the classic Western swing.

Those swing keys lie once again in the East.

WESTERN IMPACT

As we approach impact, let's do so first from the traditional point of view. So, it's back to the range and a study of the classic Western swing.

A Front View

Several positioning components—namely, the feet, knees, hands, and body alignment—are best studied from a front view (fig. 4.1).

Feet

Your left foot must be flat on the ground. If your heel lifts even a little, it's a red flag—your hip girdle is rotating too quickly. This means that your balance center is moving upward instead of staying grounded.

Your right foot should be positioned so that the ball of your foot is the only part touching the ground. If your foot remains flat at impact, you're in trouble. Your weight will stay too centered or will favor your right side, preventing you from moving smoothly over to your left. This will make you unbalanced

FIGURE 4.1 IMPACT, DRIVER—FRONT VIEW

and unable to produce pure, strong impact.

Knees

Your left knee should have a slight amount of flex and should bend toward the target. Once your club strikes the ball and moves through impact, your left knee will straighten out, but until you've made contact, your knee must stay flexed. If it doesn't, all kinds of trouble—rotational trouble—will take over. For instance, when players encourage too much rotation in their hips, they suffer from a left knee malfunction, making it straighten out too early. This can cause a wide spectrum of problems, including pulled shots and poor weight transfer.

There is also the problem of a player who bends his or her left knee too much toward the target. Smooth body rotation cannot take place for this golfer because the hips are sliding much farther than is necessary. This can cause countless technical problems, with shanks and shots curving to the right as strong possibilities.

Your right knee should bend inward several inches, allowing your right foot to turn onto the ball of the foot. The right knee poses a particular problem for an upper body player because this type of golfer tends to have his or her body weight centered—equally distributed on both legs—at impact. This immobilizes the right knee and it cannot move inward at all. For proper impact, you can't let this happen.

Hands

Your hands must be positioned slightly ahead of the ball at impact for all of your irons. For your woods, your hands will arrive just behind the ball.

The proper placement of your hands as you strike the ball is essential. Without the right alignment, you can't produce the correct angle of attack. The classic swing with your irons—all of them—requires a descending angle of attack. If your hands are where they should be, slightly ahead of the ball at impact, simple physics will force your club in a downward direction.

With your woods, you have to create a slightly upward angle of attack because those clubs have very little loft compared to your irons. The last thing you want is a downward clubhead motion getting under your shots and draining valuable distance. So, your hands must be just behind the ball at impact with your woods.

Upper and Lower Body Alignments

As you now know, your upper and lower body alignments are the pillars of a balanced swing. In the classic impact for irons, your upper torso must be stacked over your lower body every time. If you create any side-bending to the right with your upper body, you should be prepared for some blundered shots. Most commonly, this error produces an exaggerated amount of hand activity that is a desperate attempt to rescue the swing.

On the other hand, with your woods, your upper torso may lean slightly to the right. Why is this allowed? Because it leads the clubhead into an upward angle of attack, which is necessary for long shots down the fairway.

A Side View of Impact

We are going to examine several other elements of the classic Western impact from another vantage point—a side view (fig. 4.2). I don't want you to think that we are

FIGURE 4.2 IMPACT, DRIVER—SIDE VIEW

back on the Eastern path yet. The side view still examines the traditional Western swing.

Hip Girdle

Your hip girdle is one of the major power sources in your swing. If your hips have overrotated at impact, you will tap only a portion of your true power output. You need to remember that your body creates power and speed through rotation. The turning motion of your hip girdle is a natural process—and it's a rare occurrence when I have a student who doesn't automatically fire those hips over. Your job is to store that precious commodity so that it releases fully at impact.

Your transition is where you determine how your hips will react through your downswing and impact. If you begin the downswing with a slight lateral shift with your body, you increase the odds of turning your hips properly through impact. But if you start your downswing with a twisting motion, your hips will have fully turned at impact. You don't want this: it means not only that you have severely cut your swing's power, but also that your shot will probably curve toward the rough, water, a bunker, or anywhere else you don't want it to go. There are better ways to travel from tee to green than that route.

Another key to remember about your swing's path from transition to impact is that your hips will rotate more when you swing any of your longer clubs. Since your woods have the longest shafts, you swing them at the fastest speeds. For most players, it's over 90 MPH. With that in mind, you should be aware that your hips will be positioned in a more open (or rotated) position with the woods and a more closed position with your short irons. Natural law tells us "more speed, more twist."

The bottom line is that if you can delay the rotation of your hip girdle until the moment of impact, you will hit the ball cleaner, longer, and straighter.

Shoulders

From a side view of the shoulders at impact, we can examine how much they have rotated. They rotate similarly to the hip girdle. By this, I mean that you must work to slow down your rotation so that your stored power can release at impact. Since most of your upper body strength surges from the torso, you instinctively activate this power. But the task for players of all skill levels isn't just to activate their upper torso's power, but to coordinate the ensuing surge. It is not only the high handicapper who battles this problem—even the finest professionals must monitor their shoulder rotation.

Because your upper and lower body must work in a unified movement, the closer they are aligned to each other at impact, the more powerful and clean your shot will be.

Most players have a tendency to turn their hips more than their upper torso/shoulders. If you fall into this category, your timing and balance will suffer, and valuable power will be drained from impact. If, on the other hand, you have a swing shape that's dominated by your upper body, you will suffer the same consequences of poor balance and lost power when it comes to hitting the ball.

You must attempt to position your shoulders parallel to the target line (or facing the ball) at impact. If you can't, just get as close as possible. I do allow a slightly open (or overrotated) position, but be cautious of any extreme positions. They are hazardous to your handicap.

Waist Bend

At impact, your waist has a pivotal role to play. The amount of waist bend used in your address must remain until impact—and all the way through to your finish, for that matter. A player who has increased waist bend is moving in a downward direction; one who has decreased waist bend is moving upward. You don't want either shift in your alignment. Both can disrupt rotational flow and alter the distance of your arms to the ground.

Golfers who vary their waist bend almost always do it twice during their swing. For instance, if they move down in the backswing, they stand up in the downswing and vice versa. You can just imagine the outcome at impact. When you change your waist bend during the swing, you increase the number of motions to monitor. You know by now that you want a simplified swing that is easy to repeat—more parts, more problems.

Hands

At impact, your hands are in a higher position than at address. That is the natural result of your swing traveling in a downward and circular arc. It doesn't matter who the golfer is—everyone's swing produces a higher hand position at impact. I don't want you to dwell on this point; I simply urge you to accept that your hands will be higher as your club strikes the ball. Accept the fact that centrifugal force carries out this job and that your hands are along for the ride.

Read on, and you will see why I mention this point.

A Wise Western Step— Club-Fitting

Believe it or not, sometimes flawed impact isn't all your fault. We have all heard players muttering about how their clubs let them down, and there's an element of truth in that for many golfers. If you are going to get serious about your game, I urge you to see a qualified professional for proper club-fitting.

If your irons are producing consistently errant shots, you might have a *lie-angle* problem. This means that the striking point of your clubs might be all wrong for your personal physical traits: the length of your arms, legs, and so on. Your clubs should be tailored to your body, not to some assembly-line prototype.

Given the numerous club-fittings on which I have worked with students, it doesn't take long to count the number of standard-issue clubs I have recommended. In nearly every club-fitting session, I have measured and matched clubs that had to be customized in at least one way or another. And most of the time, several features have to be adjusted so the clubs conform to the unique build of the player. Keep in mind that your equipment should fit your swing shape—you shouldn't have to alter your swing to fit the equipment.

The sad fact is that most golfers won't take the time to get properly evaluated and, as a result, their progress is limited by the quality of their ill-fitted clubs. Length, lie angle, shaft flex, grip—they can all prove to be potent allies not only for impact, but also for the swing that gets you there.

Sequencing Your Impact

Before we head back to the dojo, we need to review in sequence everything that must unfold in the Western swing.

1. At impact, your left arm has fully straightened out, and your right elbow is slightly bent, not rigid. The downward flow of your swing, centrifugal force, automatically extends your left arm.
2. Your upper torso and lower body are stacked and square to the target line. A slightly open position is, however, acceptable.
3. Your left knee is flexed. This helps slow down your hip rotation because the flex of your knee is linked to your hip girdle. If your knee straightens

out, it will prematurely activate your hip rotation.

4. Your arm swing must reach impact with your hands near your left thigh.

This is the single most important Western reference for monitoring the unison of body rotation and arm swing. Impact is the point where a swing's smooth tempo can vanish in an instant. All too often a golfer's body rotation increases just before contact, and the arms are playing catch-up even as the clubhead meets the ball. With an overrotated body, the hands are too close to the right thigh, which tells you that your body and your arms are not going to be synchronized at impact.

Because the motion from the beginning of your downswing to impact races by in just half a second, you simply don't have time to make instant adjustments if there's a breakdown. And because the difference in arm swing distance from your right thigh to your left is a mere six to eight inches at impact, it is nearly impossible to feel whether your hands are lagging behind your body's rotation.

Let me identify the cornerstone of proper impact again. It's that important! To ensure solid impact, the result of synchronized body rotation and arm swing, you must strike the ball with your hands near the left thigh.

5. Your right leg is pivoting on the toes of your right foot. This is a great sign that proper weight transfer is taking place.

So, there you have it—classic Western impact. Once again, it's back to the dojo and to the steps that will bring your impact its ultimate yang.

EASTERN IMPACT

A truly secure posture gives you the sensation that your body weight is pulling downward. At the impact point of your golf swing, you must stay firmly planted and feel that solid downward contact. That connection is earth power, your grounding.

In the dojo, violations of this basic principle of balance can ruin a technique even before your opponent tries to counter with his or her own move. A flaw in your grounded posture weakens you, and if that flaw appears as you are taking the offensive, you are in deep trouble on the mat.

The same need for grounding applies to golfers who take the offensive when they strike the ball. Just like a martial artist whose posture isn't secure, players who struggle with grounding struggle with impact.

Grounding equals stable posture and balance—they are connected. On the course and in the dojo, they allow you to summon the fluid movement that fuels yang energy at impact. Posture and balance that are solid as a mountain unleash power from the ground up. Through the posture and balance that stacking can give you at impact, you will harness centrifugal force for maximum yang energy.

All of this brings us to the natural law of body alignments at impact. When I take off my golf shoes, put on my gi (training uniform), and step into the dojo, my clothing doesn't change how I apply natural law. My obedience to the correct arm and body positions that give my martial arts moves their full impact resembles the attention I give the body alignments I use on the golf course.

Grounding, stacking, and body alignments—these are your Eastern keys to balanced Western impact. Obey them, and they won't let you down. They will make your shots as solid as the ground beneath you.

Impact is the golfer's moment of truth. If you stay true to your Eastern guides, the truth will be Balanced Golf.

Staying Grounded

I will say it again: power comes from the ground up. Yet, when you are swinging your club into impact, you feel your body weight pulling downward. How can this be?

For the golfer, the answer has two parts. First, the strong base you established through the Horse and the Stack has grounded you by planting your feet firmly and by aligning your upper torso and lower body to absorb the strength of your feet's firm position. In this way, your entire stance, head to toe, absorbs the stability from the ground. How do you know you're connected? It's simple: you feel it in your feet. They are comfortable, rooted, and ready to anchor you at impact.

The second part of the answer to how you can absorb power from the ground up, even though secure posture creates a downward feeling, isn't really a mystery. You simply focus on the very word "grounding." The stability your feet summon up from the ground compels you to flex and bend downward to tap the same earth power stabilizing your feet. That's why you should feel like your body weight is traveling downward at impact. If you don't fight this feeling, your arms swing the club fluidly, and your upper torso and lower body stay stacked for incredible impact.

In my dojo, I have taught many budding martial artists that the combination of power from the ground up and their body weight pulling downward offers them the gift of earth power. If anyone asks me why it's so important, my answer is simple: mastery of these skills allows you to stay firmly planted on the ground while you are executing physical motion. The surface we stand on offers us a leverage point, and that point is crucial to developing power. If you're a basketball fan, you've been amazed by Michael Jordan's ability to defy gravity and soar through the air while he's dunking. But have you ever wondered how he uses the hardwood, the ground, as a personal launching pad? Now that I have asked this question, you will ask me the same one my students do: "Michael Jordan's great, but what's his connection to my golf game?" The ground is the connection. Michael uses it to get himself airborne; you need it to get your shots airborne. And you can use the ground in a way that he can't. I know that sounds hard to believe, but the fact is that Michael Jordan has to break his connection with the ground to cover distance to the hoop. However, a golfer has the luxury of maintaining contact all the way through the swing, and by doing so can generate incredible power. I'd like you, the golfer, to think about that for a moment.

Now, I have a question for you. What could be more important to a golfer than grounding for solid impact? I'll bet you can't think of an answer—I know I can't.

The dojo offers us a simple exercise that will let you feel proper grounding at impact. I call this training method Crossing Limbs.

Crossing Limbs

For any effective martial arts technique or golf swing, you cannot create firm impact without grounding. In grounding, you must obey several ironclad rules of natural law. Their interpretation for serious martial artists can get pretty intricate because of the variety of techniques and counters available. But for the golfer, who is concerned with only one strike, solid contact with the ball, I can simplify grounding's laws:

FIGURE 4.3 EXTENDED LEFT LEG AND RIGHT ARM—DIAGONAL VIEW

- If you are weighted on your front leg, which simply means that you are placing most of your weight on it, then the arm of your opposite side must be extended (fig. 4.3).
- If you are weighted on your rear leg, then the arm of your opposite side must be extended (fig. 4.4).

Extending the arm on the same side on which you are weighted results in an incorrect position (fig. 4.5–fig. 4.6).

Now, I would like you to perform the following steps:

1. Place your left leg forward and put at least 75 percent of your weight on this leg.

FIGURE 4.4 EXTENDED RIGHT LEG AND LEFT ARM—DIAGONAL VIEW

FIGURE 4.5 EXTENDED RIGHT LEG AND RIGHT ARM—DIAGONAL VIEW

FIGURE 4.6 EXTENDED LEFT LEG AND LEFT ARM—DIAGONAL VIEW

2. Extend your right arm.
3. Make sure your heels are pressing into the ground.

How does this stance feel? It should feel solid, rooted, giving you a strong sense of connectivity. Developing an awareness for this type of balanced structure is an important skill, especially during impact. Trust me, if your lower body doesn't feel solid, you are cutting off valuable power in your swing.

The stance you've just learned represents a significant principle in the martial arts. The theory teaches specific positioning of your lower and upper body limbs. If done correctly, anyone can use it to gain deeply rooted power. The premise behind this principle is that you can't be double-weighted. This simply means that one side of your body shouldn't carry your overall weight. If one side of your body has completely taken over as you contact the ball, you are off balance and so are your shots. That's why you have to keep your stance grounded and your weight stabilized.

In the stance we are discussing, you've extended your right arm, but haven't physically crossed your arms or legs. So, where's the basis for the title Crossing Limbs? Why is it so important to you, the golfer? It is simple geometry that works both in the dojo and on the tee, as the following Eastern lesson will explain.

1. Stand with your arms stretched out above your head.
2. Spread your legs slightly apart.

If I were to draw a line from your right hand down to your left foot and another line from your left hand down to your right foot, we would have the letter *X*. The X literally marks the spot—the spot of true balance. The two top points of the X represent your raised arms, the two bottom points your feet. What do these four points have in common? They cross in the X's center.

Translating that thought to your own body, what key region lies at your center? Your one-point, your balance center. This crossing principle of limbs is what allows you to maintain a truly balanced posture for your swing's impact. You have to become Mr. or Ms. X for solid contact with the ball.

Let's take this key Eastern principle one step further for your golf game. If we look at a front view of a

player making impact with his left heel raised, it's like looking at that X with one of its "feet" up—it spoils the letter's shape, or balance. On the other hand, if we look at a golfer who is tilting or leaning too far left at impact, this also violates the stance's X factor.

A golfer who reaches impact with any point out of alignment is not grounded. Any lifting of the heels or body tilting has broken both a grounded stance and a connection to the balance center, the one-point. You must accept that X does mark the spot for perfect balance at impact. That's natural law, and that's the way you must align your limbs.

The more you practice my Crossing Limbs principles, the more you will reinforce your ability to ground at impact. Through repetition, you will plant your feet comfortably and naturally, connected to earth power.

Another Crossing Limbs Connection
The key to keeping your limbs crossed and your X intact is your foot action. "Action?" you're asking. You thought I wanted your feet planted, summoning earth power.

Of course I do, so let me explain what I mean by action. You have to control your feet—your foot action at impact. You have to make your feet, particularly your heels, behave themselves as your club hits the ball. You can't allow them to ruin your X posture and cut your connection to earth power.

Beginning with the Horse at your setup, the techniques we have practiced emphasize rooting, your feet firmly on the ground. In a perfect golfing world, I would prefer no lifting of your left heel at all. A complete lack of lift smooths out your weight transfer and heads off other mechanical problems too long and painful to list. But because golf is not, as the saying goes, "a game of perfect," I've learned to accept that many players can lift their left heel just a little bit. The operative word is "little," the least possible violation to grounding.

Once you reach impact, your left heel is rooted, tapped into earth power. But, as you strike the ball, it's your other heel—the right—that lifts slightly off the ground. Don't resist. The energy of your club hitting the ball urges your right heel to lift slightly, but only slightly. So, the ideal positions for solid impact are a grounded left foot and a minimal lift with the right heel.

I guarantee that now you have another question. Since I have had you press both heels against the ground in the Crossing Limbs stance but you're allowed—grudgingly—to lift your left heel slightly in the backswing and your right heel at impact, why was that lesson from my dojo so important? This is a valid question and easily answered. Except for that instant in your backswing, your left heel must be planted from setup to impact. Crossing Limbs has shown you exactly how to root that heel. The same holds true for your right heel.

For impact, regular practice of Crossing Limbs teaches you that you can stay grounded even with minimal heel movement. Remember that you're Mr. or Ms. X, so if you are weighted on the left leg at impact, you can let loose with your right arm. But if you're weighted on the right leg at impact, you can call 911 because there will be an emergency situation as your club meets the ball. Your right arm will want to hit the ball, but being weighted on the right creates a double-weightedness in your body—and you know that the principle of

Crossing Limbs doesn't function that way.

Besides being the natural enemy of double-weightedness, Crossing Limbs can defeat the worst possible foot action by golfers—both heels off the ground at impact. This disaster generally occurs when a player's hip girdle is activated too quickly in the downswing. I have found the problem to be particularly common among women and juniors because they strain to generate more power in their swing. They fire their hips so quickly that their grounding is violated, and this furious twisting motion lifts both heels. If such airborne foot action produces a decent stroke, it's blind luck or a miracle. No golfer can rely for long on this type of action.

Remember that you must plant your feet to absorb earth power and to control the limited heel action a proper swing allows. Remember something else, too: Crossing Limbs will teach you to ground your feet and to manage your heels for clean and repeatable impact.

Body Alignments

The position of your body and arms at impact must be synchronized. Your head, your upper torso, your lower body, and your arms must obey the natural law of body alignments to create maximum power from minimal effort. For the golfer, that means maximum distance and control—if he or she maintains those key alignments into the impact zone.

The dojo has taught you that if one body component is moving or turning, so should all the others. I have said it before, but bear with me, because I have to say it again: it's hard to believe, but if one part of your body is not synchronized and aligned, your swing will collapse. Without the proper alignments, a martial artist cannot deliver a potent strike, and a golfer cannot make solid impact.

I want you to take a long look at Figures 4.7 through 4.9. Using three different martial arts applications, these pictures illustrate how correct body alignments can produce perfect impact and how flawed body alignments will torment your balance and your power output.

Now, let's apply these three lessons on impact in the dojo to impact on the course. Just as the incorrectly aligned wide-angled right strike destroyed my posture and power, a similar misalignment

FIGURE 4.7 OPEN RIGHT HAND STRIKE ON CENTERLINE—FRONT VIEW

This is exactly what the doctor ordered—a technique that adheres to the principles of body alignments and Crossing Limbs. But for our discussion, the key is that the hand technique is executed right on the centerline. This is without a doubt the most effective method for developing maximum power while keeping a solid foundation.

FIGURE 4.8 WIDE RIGHT PUNCH—FRONT VIEW

This wide-angled strike clearly shows how the principle of body alignments can be violated. As a matter of fact, this is what most beginning martial arts students do when they enter the dojo. However, after many hours of training, a practitioner will realize just how faulty this type of movement can be.

FIGURE 4.9 DOUBLE HAND PARRY—DIAGONAL VIEW

The double hand parry is a technique used to deflect incoming strikes. There are many variations; however, you will notice that the one I'm using is done on my centerline. That's because it's the most effective and the safest version.

will ruin the golfer's impact. Figures 4.10 through 4.12 show how you can identify optimal positions and recognize problem spots.

Keep in mind that if you cannot produce the correct body alignments at impact, it's like driving a car with a flat tire. You won't get far. Not a happy picture, is it?

What does create a pretty image is picture-perfect impact. Thanks to East and West meeting at your point of impact—the ball—you possess the grounding, the lateral movement, and the alignments to strike the ball with a smooth flow of yang energy each and every time.

FIGURE 4.10 IMPACT (CORRECT), 6-IRON—FRONT VIEW

This figure shows the ideal impact position. The arms and body have worked together as a unit, and now—it's a moot point—solid impact is inevitable.

FIGURE 4.11 IMPACT (ARMS NEAR RIGHT LEG), 6-IRON—FRONT VIEW

This golfer will produce many bad shots that include some pretty wild slices. You can see that he is striking the ball with his arms near his right leg. This means that his body turned much too quickly in the downswing and that his arms just couldn't catch up.

FIGURE 4.12 IMPACT (ARMS CROSSED, NO BODY TWIST) 6-IRON—FRONT VIEW

Our last player is someone who has very little body motion and mainly uses his arms. You can see that his arms have crossed his upper body and have traveled past his left leg. This type of misalignment usually causes pulled and/or hooked shots.

SUMMARY

Although the force of yang has carried you through impact, this Eastern energy isn't done with you yet—and you will be glad it isn't. It is going to take you into your swing's final key elements: the follow-through and finish. But, don't get overconfident. There is still work to be done if you want your swing to finish with the same balance with which it began on its Eastern path.

5

THE FOLLOW-THROUGH AND FINISH— THE FINAL ACT

When you welcomed yin into your setup and yielded to yang through-out your backswing, downswing, and impact, you followed the path of Balanced Golf. Now, yang must finish what it started in your swing.

Over the years, I have helped a lot of students whose swings started strong but faltered as they moved through impact and into the follow-through and finish. Most of us have winced as parents or teachers have thrown that old adage "finish what you started" our way. You probably wish I would put that "command" in some other words. But as annoying as the saying is, for the golfer it's absolutely true. You must follow every step from setup to finish if you want to control your swing and lower your handicap. Finish what you started—there's no escaping it in the golf swing.

As a matter of fact, I encourage all my students to pay attention to

their finish position. It is a great indicator of problems that may have arisen during your swing. Because I or even your playing partner can't *see* what your club is doing at impact, it's always best to check where your body and the club finish once you've hit the ball. The naked eye just isn't equipped to pick up the subtleties of a club moving through impact. That's why a high-speed video camera is such an asset when you are fine-tuning your golf swing. You can freeze-frame your body motions and see exactly how the club is positioned.

It is amazing what information your finish position will provide. For instance, if you alter your waist bend and come out of a shot, your shoulders will be off-kilter and you will have poor balance. On the other hand, if you use excessive hand and forearm rotation through the ball, the club will be positioned way to the left as you complete your swing. So, you see, your finish is really an insightful teacher. Strike a pose and try to hold your finish. Look around at all your body parts and the club; they just might be trying to tell you something.

THE WESTERN FOLLOW-THROUGH AND FINISH

Upper and Lower Body Alignment

The end of your swing must maintain correct body alignments for balance. As you move from impact to finish, your upper torso and lower body straighten. If you lean back on your right side or form what's known as a reverse C position, I'll bet you've made poor contact with the ball. That's because your weight transfer hasn't come far enough left and because you're straining your lower back.

I would like to see 80 percent of your weight on a straight left leg at finish. Don't agonize over what 80 percent feels like. You will know you're balanced if you can feel most of your weight on your left leg. I always tell my students that they

should be able to lift their right foot when they complete their finish. If you can't, not enough body weight shifted during the swing.

A look at a baseball pitching mound is useful here. Watch as a good pitcher reaches his follow-through and finish. A right-hander ends up with virtually all of his weight on his left leg—the same left leg a golfer weights in the finish. Yet the pitcher doesn't lose his balance. Even though his right leg is in the air for a moment or two—not what we want in the golf swing—he has maintained just enough weight on his right side to keep him from toppling over. The point is that in rotational motion, most of a right-handed athlete's weight must end up on his left leg at the follow-through and finish.

Let's look to another sport for an example of weight displacement with the upper torso and lower body. When tennis players have time to set up on the baseline and rip a cross-court forehand, they transfer most of their weight to the left leg at the stroke's follow-through and finish. If they didn't move through the shot with this type of motion, there would be much less speed, and anyone could return their shot.

FIGURE 5.1 JUST PAST IMPACT AND INTO FINISH POSITION, DRIVER—FRONT VIEW

Right Foot

In the golf swing's finish, your right foot position is a cardinal element. If you remain flat-footed, you have a problem: you've executed your rotation and weight shift poorly. This, in turn, means that your contact was almost guaranteed to be flawed. I know you've hit a bad shot because flat-footedness indicates that you have centered your weight—equal distribution on each leg—in your swing. Too much centering, which means that you've divided your weight equally too deep into your swing, has allowed your upper torso to take over and to disturb your rotation. If you're feeling flat-footed, you're not swinging the club with balance and power.

How can you correct this problem for a smooth finish and follow-through? You have to pivot on the toes of your right foot. This will guide your hips for the proper range of motion and let you finish strong.

Right Shoulder and Right Hip

I use the right shoulder and right hip as reference points when I have students who overrotate their bodies through impact and onward. The common checkpoint for both is an alignment to the original ball position. If your right hip and shoulder turn in front of the ball—toward the target—you diminish your ability to control your shots' direction. Although I have had observant students point out that Seve Ballesteros and Vijay Singh use overrotated positions, I offer two rebuttals. The first is familiar to you by now: guys like that possess an enormous amount of natural talent that no one else can mimic, let alone duplicate. My second response is that in recent years Seve and Vijay have both worked to overcome overrotation. Why? It's simple—even the finest players are always seeking better control of their shots. I had the opportunity to spend quite a bit of time with Seve as Mac O'Grady was correcting some of Seve's swing flaws. I can tell you firsthand that the results were remarkable when Seve mastered this finish position.

To be quite candid, I want to emphasize that the positions of your right shoulder and hip apply more to the advanced or intermediate golfer than to the beginner. Because I don't want the beginner to do anything to hinder the downswing's motion through impact and into finish, I don't stress the right shoulder and hip position. Only if a new player overrotates so unnaturally that it can't be ignored do I consider increasing his or her awareness of these positions during the swing.

Because more experienced players have greater mindfulness of their body positions, I am on the lookout to see whether they are rotating excessively. I do this because once a player has a decent swing, it's no longer necessary for the shoulders and hips to turn too much through impact. As a matter of fact, for chronic overrotators, I work to establish a breaking of body rotation—but only after the club has traveled several feet past impact. At this stage, a player learns to simply fold the arms upward into a natural finish as body rotation smoothly adjusts.

A Western Checklist for the Follow-through

1. Your head begins to rotate to the left and out toward the target.
2. Your right and left arms are extended down the target line, with the club shaft positioned similarly to your right arm. If the shaft is more vertical at this

point, it reflects too much hand action, a fatal move for proper follow-through. This condition will cause you to have limited body movement and produce a wide variety of shots, including thin ones, heavy ones, and the dreaded hooks.

3. Both of your arms—along with your upper torso and lower body—are rotating through impact together. This creates a unified motion so that your arms and body face in the same direction during the follow-through.
4. Your body weight has predominantly shifted onto your left leg.

A Western Checklist for the Finish

1. Your upper torso and left leg have formed a straight line. Your entire back is also straight.
2. Your head has rotated fully toward the target.
3. Your left leg supports 80 percent of your weight.
4. Your arm swing and club have finished in a completed high position.
5. Your right shoulder and right hip are aiming at the original ball location. The positions of

your right shoulder and hip give you road signs to proper body rotation. If these two reference points are out of place, your swing is not under control.

6. Your right foot has rotated onto your toes. This signals that your weight has shifted properly to the left side.

That is how you follow through with and finish the classic Western swing. But, as even the world's best players acknowledge, finishing what you've started on the course is sometimes easier said than done.

THE EASTERN PATH

In the dojo, the martial artist welcomes yang into all movements—all the way to the end. Whether delivering a punch, a kick, or a parry, he or she learns that the force of yang must be allowed to finish not only an opponent, but also the technique itself. Once martial artists recognize that they must carry out their moves completely from start to finish or their motion becomes unbalanced and depleted of strength, they discover a real eye-opener: if you don't interrupt the flow of yang, any

maneuver will be completed naturally and powerfully. Finishing what they have started becomes effortless.

A useful illustration I share with my martial arts students can also be applied to your golf swing. I urge them to hit through any intended target. This ensures that the yang energy they have used to launch a technique doesn't get cut off short. If, for instance, they were aiming at the chest, I tell them to imagine that the attacker's back is really the target. This encourages a full body technique and allows them to create more power. If they were to stop short and retract their strike, the technique would have only minimal effect.

This striking-through motion also encourages something called *ki extension*, which comes from the teachings of ki principles. In a nutshell, it is your ability to extend the focus of your mind past the target. It usually takes some time to develop this ability, but once it's honed, there are some significant advantages.

By hitting through during impact with your club, you are already using a form of ki extension. So, don't get in the way; just let the club move smoothly through as it sends your ball for a ride into the wild blue yonder.

Weight Transfer

I teach both my martial arts and golf students that we are engineered to regulate lateral force. I know this because natural law has already set prerequisites for us to follow. As a matter of fact, every move on the mat, no matter which Eastern system I'm discussing, focuses on fluid motion. To execute proper kicks and punches, controlling necessary weight transfer into a move's final phase is crucial. If students don't perform this properly, it tells me two things: they won't effectively finish their strike; and the impact of their techniques won't deliver full power. How do I know that their impact will be depleted? I know because their physical motions following impact don't lie. A mismanaged yang force—something in weight transfer, stacking, and/or body alignments—has triggered a poor follow-through and finish. That is how I know that potential power has been consumed the wrong way. The bad finish just confirms everything.

The same principle applies to you, the golfer. In a balanced swing's follow-through and finish, yang smoothly transfers your weight to the left. This allows your stacking and your body alignments to do their job, which is to keep you balanced and connected all the way into your swing's conclusion. But if you throw up any barrier, no matter how subtle, to yang as it transfers your weight to the left, you are breaking the energy current for a complete swing. Weight transfer, stacking, body alignments—these three Eastern allies must be obeyed for you to finish the balanced, powerful swing that you want.

Precise Athletic Motion— the Martial Arts Way

For movements in the dojo, the force of yang transfers your weight with no strain—but only if you don't resist. I have learned from several renowned masters of the martial arts that anything you do to hamper this natural exchange of weight in motion prevents you from carrying a move to its inherent conclusion. The key to a strong martial arts follow-through and finish is recognizing and controlling weight transfer.

My Eastern training has proven to me that a flawed finish is a warning signal to something else having broken down earlier in a movement. The key word here is "movement." My conviction is that, as the martial arts teach, weight transfer is a bonafide athletic motion. Through years of practicing and perfecting my moves on the mat, I have grasped that weight transfer and lateral motion are united. I have learned that if I don't shift my weight right or left at the appropriate moment, an astute martial artist will exploit that weakness of movement to take over the encounter. Because a critical weight transfer in martial arts maneuvers unfolds as you progress through impact and into follow-through and finish, you must not be fooled into thinking that impact alone is your means to an end. You are still vulnerable—your foe on the mat will be happy to finish you if you don't complete the move and if you don't change your weight transfer.

For the golfer, problems can also erupt at the very instant your club strikes ball and follow-through begins. For example, if your weight stays too centered, equal on both legs, there's trouble ahead. Odds are, you will probably have poor contact and send the ball curving way off to the right or left. Why? Because you are allowing your hands to become overly active and you are forcing your body to twist like there's no tomorrow.

I want to bring you back to those words "weight movement" again. Here's where an Eastern principle of Balanced Golf again challenges conventional Western teaching. My view, the culmination of more than two decades in the dojo, is that the golf swing's weight transfer—not only to the left as a player moves into the follow-through and finish, but also to the right during the backswing—is a true athletic motion. Some of my PGA teaching colleagues advocate the traditional Western view of a golf swing that uses a fixed position, or one rotational point. I would agree with them if we were steel machines; however, that's not the case. I have many friends on Tour who subscribe to this methodology, and I don't utter a word to change their minds. But I do have two main disputes with folks who try to use this one-pointed rotation or fixed axis. The first is that it clearly stresses the body more; by resisting the natural flow of your body you strain more body parts, especially the lower back. Talk to a few people who use this method, and I'm sure that somewhere in your conversation, they will mention that they have a painful back. Second, if you watch any player using this fixed axis style, on slow-motion video, you'll see that he or she moves a little to the right in the backswing and a little to the left in the downswing. Case closed! I will even go out on a limb here and say that all world-class players move to their right on the backswing and to their left in the downswing. Some may move more than others, but they all move.

By trying to resist this natural motion, you're just making it more difficult for yourself and adding to the possibility of some sort of injury. In Western terms, it's athletic motion in the purest sense. Don't avoid it.

Stacked for the Finish

A properly stacked finish position will prove to you that consistent ball-striking ability isn't just a coincidence. By getting yourself into this ideal position, you'll not only see great results, but you also can practice much longer than you ever

did before. Why? Because there will be an ease of motion in all of the integrated body parts of your swing. This means you can hit those extra balls and smooth out any problems that have come up without feeling too fatigued. Sign me up for that program!

Figures 5.2 through 5.5 show the proper and improper positions for impact and finish.

FIGURE 5.2 IMPACT (CORRECT), 6-IRON—FRONT VIEW
You can see here that my body is stacked and ready for action. What I want you to pay particular attention to is how my upper and lower body are staying over one another. This position gives you the best possible chance of making solid contact.

FIGURE 5.3 IMPACT (INCORRECT; SIDE BEND TO THE RIGHT), 6-IRON—FRONT VIEW

You can see here that there is far too much side bending with my upper torso. I want you to see this specific position because it's one of the most common errors at impact. If you drew a line from my belt buckle to the top of my head, you would see just how severe this angle is. Now compare it to the one in Figure 5.2, and see the difference.

FIGURE 5.4 FINISH (CORRECT), 6-IRON—FRONT VIEW

This is obviously the ideal finish position. Look at how straight my left side is positioned—my left leg and upper torso form one straight line. When I see a golfer coming close to this position, I know he or she has made a good pass at the ball.

FIGURE 5.5 FINISH (INCORRECT; REVERSE C POSITION), 6-IRON—FRONT VIEW

It hurts for me to even look at this position. I can already feel the pain in my lower back, how about you? This leaning back motion is quite common. As a matter of fact, most average players use this sort of action. When I was a junior golfer, this type of posture was really advocated. It's a good thing that teaching methods have evolved to eliminate this kind of positioning.

Summary

In my career as both a PGA instructor and master-level martial artist, I have determined that the finished product of physical motions reveals very important ingredients to a student's effectiveness. Not only are the setup and the swinging motion consequential, but so is the way that you arrive at the completion of your movement. This means that you must flow through impact with an effortless motion and allow your own athletic ability to play a significant role in your swing. Remember, the finish is your report card—shoot for an A+.

PART II

STAYING ON THE PATH
OF BALANCED GOLF

6

TURNING ON YOUR POWER SOURCES

In Part I, I revealed the simple Eastern principles that took you step by step from setup through finish. Now it's time to refine and enhance your new ability to bring fluid yin and yang into your swing. We are going to "turn on" your Western power sources through another principle from the East called *new motions*.

Incorporating unfamiliar motions into any walk of life can be a major task, but that is especially true in the golf swing because we're dealing with body motion and rotational speed. It is also especially true at this point on our journey because we are going to take a look at your swing's desired rotation and speed in ways that you've never encountered—Eastern ways.

Rotational motion and speed are the very core of a balanced swing's yin and yang, and if you accept the wisdom of the Eastern guides you're

about to meet, I promise they will bring you the repeatable and powerful swing you've always craved. Your handicap will go down and your enjoyment of the game will soar as far as your drives!

Previously, I had you focus on Eastern movements that grounded, stacked, and synchronized your swing so that your movements work in unison, flowing and aligned from head to toe. Exercises such as Body Rotations I and II have allowed you to feel proper rotational movement and to simulate the correct timing—synchronization—of your swing. Remember, timing equals tempo. You know this, you've felt it. Now, we are going to explore the connection between your power sources and how they combine to switch on maximum yang—maximum energy flow, power, and speed—and do so in the way that's right for you.

As I taught you simple martial arts in our previous lessons, we isolated each key segment of the swing: the setup, the backswing, the transition and downswing, impact, and the follow-through and finish. Our body rotation exercises gave you a sense of flow and rhythm, and now it is time to guarantee that you don't sacrifice this fluid motion for too much speed. What I mean is that you hold the keys to unforced yang; you don't have to force rotational speed for more power. Your four major power sources—your hip girdle, your upper torso, your arms, and your wrists—will provide all the energy, or yang, you will ever need. But the kicker here is that you must let all four sources flow together for a simultaneous release at impact. You can't let one of these sources surge so much that it throws the others out of alignment. Any motion that jolts the flow ruins the proper speed, no matter how fast or slow the tempo required, of any movement. If you are hammering a nail into a wall, you line up the nail and use just enough pressure to bang it in with several strikes. If you try to knock it in with one shot, there's a good chance you'll drive the nail in crooked. Why? Because your sudden and unnecessary burst of force—yang—was improper for the task.

Let's get into your car for a more distinct example of forced speed that does no one any good. You are driving to the course along a road where the posted speed limit is forty-five, and you come to a stop at a red light. As the light turns green, do you slam your power source, the gas pedal, as hard as possible to get back up to forty-five immediately? If you do, I'm sure glad I'm not in the passenger seat. My guess is that your car is all over the road and that you're fighting to control the wheel. The point is that if you accelerate smoothly, you will reach forty-five at the proper moment. Everything is under control. Similarly, if you're changing lanes on the highway, you don't normally slam down the gas pedal—not if you want to increase your car's motion smoothly! You shouldn't try to force speed, and nowhere is that truer than in your golf swing.

Let's get out of the car, and head back to the practice tee to discuss your game's power sources.

POWER FROM THE WEST

As I mentioned earlier, there are four major power sources in your golf swing:

- Hip girdle
- Upper torso
- Arm speed
- Wrists

These four key sources are the points where you transfer raw energy into explosive but now controlled power. In the classic swing, you synchronize these four sources for simultaneous release at impact. When you can do this, you're ensuring proper body motion and coordination for all of them.

In their most basic context, the four power sources are the pillars of power in your Western swing. If they don't hold up, your swing won't hold up. This is why synchronization of these elements is so crucial. And what is the most important component in synchronization? In a word, timing. If you time, or sequence, all four power sources to flow together smoothly, you will have a swing that can stand up under any conditions. That's what I mean by a repeatable routine!

Whether we are talking about a heavy hitter like John Daly or Tiger Woods, or a finesse player like Tom Kite, their swings all have something in common: all four power sources switch on together at impact. Obviously, Tom will rarely drive a ball like John or Tiger, but Tom's mastery of simultaneous release does produce the maximum results for his physique. Those results have been terrific, allowing him to compete with the long-distance guys on Tour. No matter what your own body type is, the united synergy of your four power sources can be timed to give you the distance, the balance, and the control that come with a harmonious release at impact. You can achieve your own "personal best," and what more could any golfer of any level want?

Problems in Your Western Power Plant

To keep your Western power sources on-line, you must be aware of the problems and breakdowns that can arise in each one and can prevent them from working together. So, here is a more detailed look at your power sources.

Hip Girdle

It's okay to shake and swivel your hips on the dance floor, but any misplaced hip motion in your golf swing will lead you nowhere, except maybe into bogey territory.

If you have a small or even medium frame, you really have to pay attention to your hips because you're the most likely candidate to turn to them for help—the wrong kind of help. Seeking more power in their swings, smaller players try to create more club speed by snapping their hips into impact. It's a terrible tactic that fuels overrotation for an unbalanced swing. Since you can't reach your maximum distance if you're unbalanced, any yardage that an overrotated swing might seem to offer just camouflages your flaw. And not for long.

You must keep in mind that your hips have a limited range of rotation, and once they've turned their given distance, that's all the power they can produce. So, in developing lower body control and awareness, you want to have the ability to use the power in your hips when you see

fit. An ideal scenario in the downswing would be a delayed action in their turning motion so that power can be stored—like a spring can be tightened down. Then, once the club is about to strike the ball, you let loose, and the spring uncoils like a rocket.

I have found that it's almost impossible for juniors and many women players to avoid the excessive twisting motion that their hips naturally create. I certainly understand why they do: the hips are a strong power source and their overrotation does force a very aggressive downswing. But it's a downswing that's literally downhill for your game. Aggression has to be controlled, and the only way to keep your hips from betraying your swing is to control them. That's why their motion must be timed along with the other power sources.

One of the worst traits that overly aggressive hip rotation spins into your game is to pull your heels off the ground several inches, wrecking your stance, your alignments, everything. Again, happy feet and heels might be fine on the dance floor, but not on the golf course.

The only way to stop those hips from firing too strongly is to synchronize them with the other three power sources—the upper torso, the arms, and the wrists.

Upper Torso

Your upper torso is perhaps the most misunderstood and most abused power source of them all. In my years as a PGA instructor, I've discovered that young and middle-aged men generally rely too heavily on their upper torsos for rotational speed. There is actually a logical reason behind this flaw: because a lot of guys are pretty strong through their chest and shoulders, they turn to this natural power source for increased speed and distance. At least that's what they think they're doing, consciously or subconsciously. In reality, they are following a false guide here—the speed and the yardage they think they're generating are actually the by-products of overrotation. They may think that they're pounding the ball, but the effort they are demanding from their upper torso is way out of line. When I have brought up this point with a lot of upper body players, they're confused at first and

defend their unbalanced swings by saying something like this: "But didn't I just crush my last drive?"

"Yeah, you did," I have to admit sometimes. But then I ask them a pair of questions. "Are your drives that long consistently?" "Are your drives consistently straight?"

Now, as I spot doubt in their eyes, I pose one more question, one that gets to the core of any long hitter's makeup. "Do you often hit a booming shot that's followed by another in which you swing just as hard, but get far less yardage?"

If you answered "no" to my first two questions and "yes" to my third, I'm willing to bet that you're generating too much juice from your upper torso. The hard truth is that you are overrotating.

What makes this a tricky problem for any instructor and student hinges on two factors. The first, as I've pointed out, is the natural inclination of a golfer wanting to turn to his upper torso for strength; the second is that even if you swing the club with perfect balance and tempo from takeaway to transition, you can lose it all in the downswing because the upper torso switches on too much energy and disrupts the four-way flow of your power sources at impact. Instead of a simultaneous release of all four as your club strikes the ball, you have one power source—the upper torso—working against the other three. That's why even if an upper body player crushes the occasional tape-measure drive, he or she will never do it consistently. I guarantee that if you're this type of golfer, your upper torso power surges are adding strokes to your scorecard. What good are bragging rights to the longest drive in your foursome if you are carding the highest scores? Especially when less upper body strain will work toward the simultaneous motions that give your impact more power and more consistency.

For those of you still thinking that because your upper body strength is so great, you have to use it as hard and as fast as possible, I think a quick field trip from the course to the baseball diamond can really illustrate my point. You have probably heard the expression "he swings from the heels." If you think about when you've heard announcers use these words, they usually refer to a hitter who has just taken a ferocious cut, whiffing completely

and stumbling around the batter's box at his swing's finish. He has given free reign to his upper torso, and it has taken over his swing. In its worst scenario, this sudden forward jolt creates a lunging swing and upsets the entire stance—just like it would for a golfer. Once in a very great while, a Mark McGwire or a Mo Vaughn can swing from their heels and knock one into the bleachers, but if you watch when they or most sluggers really connect, their swings are seamless. Everything almost looks too easy—fluid motion. That's because most of the time great hitters and great golfers synchronize their power sources. Over the long haul, overrotation of the upper torso is a recipe for fruitless, inconsistent results in any athletic motion where rotational speed is key.

When it comes to the upper torso, there is a principle that guides proper motion whether we're talking about Tiger Woods ripping a long drive, Roger Clemens firing a 98-MPH fastball, or Andre Agassi crushing a baseline forehand. All three athletes share this upper body principle: each one's upper torso is synchronized to turn slightly ahead of the arm—or arms, in Tiger's case. If the upper torso drags your arms too far behind, the release of your power sources will be off. For the golfer, this means dissipated power and errant shots.

Just let your upper torso align itself with the structure of your lower body—and let them both turn and release at the same speed. This will certainly make it easier for the last two power sources to blend into this type of action.

Speed of Arms

Once again, any discussion of the swing's proper speed must begin with that familiar warning—too much speed kills. The speed of your arms dictates the rhythm and pace of your swing. The distance you generate with each club in your bag depends on how fast your arms are moving the club, and this is where golfers of all ages, shapes, and sizes make a disastrous detour. Rather than letting the length of the club lead them to the proper speed, they try to accelerate, or to force, the club. It's not a good idea. For example, a skilled player generates speeds of about 105 MPH with the driver and about 95 MPH with the 5-iron.

Although there is a 10 MPH drop-off in speed, the player is actually swinging both clubs at a consistent tempo. It is just that the club lengths are dictating the speed, as they should.

Here is how I teach this essential concept. Pick up your driver, and take a few practice swings. Now, do the same with a 5-iron and then a 7-iron. The tempo—the way your arms are moving the club—should feel essentially the same regardless of which club you swing. From sand wedge to driver, normal speed increments go up about 3 MPH with each club. The longer the club, the faster it will move, without you even having to make any forceful adjustments with your arms. Don't worry about trying to visualize that internal speedometer for your clubs. All you have to remember is that each club, in its own way, has a built-in speedometer. It knows exactly how fast to go.

How hard and how fast should your arms swing the club? Most golfers have grappled with this question. At some point, everyone who picks up a club gets it in their heads to swing as hard and as fast as they can. For most players, this urge is at its worst the first few swings they ever take. When I was a kid taking my first few whacks at a ball, I have to admit that I, too, threw every ounce into each swing. However, I quickly got the message: calm down your movements and your swing. Let your body and the club do their work!

I think a great example of arm speed control has to be from the PGA Tour. If you can recall the last televised tournament you watched, I bet you cannot name one player who swung as hard as he could. Most of the time, I hear comments along this line: "Can you believe how effortlessly he's swinging?" Every PGA Tour player I have ever spoken to has said that they try to swing using only 80 percent of their arm speed. I think that should send you a clear message—if maximum arm speed were truly beneficial, then the best players in the world would be employing it.

So, take a lesson from them and me. Keep your arm speed under control.

Wrists

The fourth power source, your wrists, will open the door to explo-

sive energy. In coordination with your arms, your wrists can create additional but unforced clubhead speed. Done properly, we're talking about lots of yardage here.

"Properly," of course, is the critical word. Your arms can produce only part of the necessary speed in the golf swing. If you don't allow your wrists to do their job, to hinge, and you strain to keep them too rigid, you will limit the movement of your club. And you don't have to tighten them much to drain valuable speed. Here's proof: take your normal swing from setup to transition, but keep your wrists stiff. It feels completely awkward, doesn't it?

Now, go ahead and swing into your finish with this stiff-wristed swing. Feel that? It's even more uncomfortable when you move from your downswing through impact. Your wrists are trying to tell you something. If you don't allow them to hinge, your swing becomes strained and slower. That is not the ideal combination for distance and control.

As with your other three power sources, though, you cannot allow your wrists to move so much and so quickly that they ruin the simultaneous release of your four-way energy. They must be linked to work in unison with your hip girdle, your upper torso, and your arms.

If you overuse or underuse your wrists in your downswing, you will deplete their beneficial power before the club even gets to the ball. Earlier, we discussed the lag position. This is exactly how the wrists contribute power to your swing. The lag holds and stores this force so that the club can be released dynamically at just the right time—impact. If you let this power source activate prematurely, say good-bye to your extra mileage off the tee.

Remember that if any other power source malfunctions, the energy from your wrists (for speed) will dwindle, and your swing will suffer.

There they are—your four major Western power sources and the things that can short-circuit simultaneous release. Speed through proper rotation is the glue of any balanced golf swing, and we will firm that up with a trip to the dojo, where the martial arts principle of new motions holds the key to a

mutual release of your power sources.

THE EASTERN SWITCHES TO YOUR WESTERN POWER SOURCES

Whether you are learning the golf swing, a kick, or a punch, you are experiencing *new motions*, the movements of a beginner. All new physical motion can and usually does feel clumsy, sometimes for quite a while. It is particularly hard for my new golf and martial arts students to discover that even though they are well coordinated, that alone doesn't mean they can master a particular move as quickly as they would like. They are not used to feeling out of sync. Students soon accept that they have to learn the fundamentals of new motions. Just because a Greg Norman or a Mark O'Meara makes hitting a golf ball look easy or because a martial arts master performs the most intricate moves quickly and fluidly, doesn't mean those movements are easy. The awkwardness that students experience tells them the hard truth:

they can't hope to perform any new motion at a high level until they have mastered every subtlety of that motion through practice, practice, and more practice. Ease of movement comes through repetition of the fundamentals. In the dojo and on the course, there is simply no other way.

The key to mastering new motions—whether in the martial artist's stances, strikes, kicks, and parries or the golfer's setup, backswing, and downswing—is to turn new motions into old ones. By "old," I mean that you practice them enough to listen to your body's power sources, which guide your movements. At first, they will tell you that it's alright to feel clumsy when you learn any new action. Then, slowly, the movements begin to feel more comfortable. Before you know it, you are performing the tasks easily and efficiently. And because the same power sources of the golf swing rule countless movements in the dojo, the way I teach new motions to my martial arts students is the perfect approach for showing not only swing mechanics to novice golfers, but also for zeroing in on proper power source usage for players of any skill level.

The core of teaching new motions on the course or on the mat is to magnify every movement. New motions have to be executed in long and wide movements. To truly grasp what any new action is all about, you must exaggerate every element of it; by performing the motion in a long, wide manner, you experience every possible sequence of that movement. It's a lot like the old saying that you have to walk before you run. In a very real sense, when I'm working with golfers or martial arts students, I walk them through every move. As we practice the move again and again, I allow the students to decrease the exaggerated movement as they become more proficient. Eventually, we arrive at the precise motion required, and because the students have experienced every possible length and width of the move, they understand the proper range of motion. With that understanding comes repeatable motion, the essentials of a skilled golfer and a skilled martial artist alike.

I can assure you that the magnified approach to length and width in martial arts movements will work for your golf swing. You simply can't understand athletic motion until you have experienced it both long and wide *and* short and sweet.

I am not so sure "sweet" describes how I felt about this martial arts technique at first. Early on in my Eastern training, I was thrown around by my master teachers, and, as I picked myself up off the mat, I didn't even realize what had happened. My teachers' moves were so effortless and precise that they seemed undetectable. Then, as these masters took me through new motions in a long, wide manner and eventually narrowed each move to its powerful essence, exaggeration gave way to proficiency. In time, I realized that I could magnify each element of the golf swing in the same manner.

One reason the long, wide approach works so beautifully in both the dojo and on the course is that the essence of both disciplines is the creation of speed through rotation. The word "rotation" itself denotes circular movement. Because natural law teaches that the human body is engineered for circular motion and that any movement you make is circular in nature, any attempt you make to move a joint in a straight, or linear, manner violates natural law. Here's where the tech-nique of exaggerated movement— long and wide—comes in: as you refine your skill in side-to-side (lateral) motion, you shrink the width of your rotation from a wide circle to a smaller one. This Eastern approach to new motions will let you magnify your swing so that you can narrow it to its most balanced and powerful essence.

Now, it's time for you to feel what the long and wide approach to new motions can do for your golf swing and what exaggeration can do to cultivate new motions into polished movement. Figure 6.1 through Figure 6.4 demonstrate the difference between the new motions approach to martial arts movements and the same movements after experience has been acquired.

New Motions and the Golf Swing

Aren't you glad that balanced golf doesn't require you to take a tumble like my partner in the wrist-lock maneuver? Next, we're going to apply the same Eastern principles of new motions to your golf swing. I have decided to focus on lateral movement and the way we can train it using this theory (fig. 6.5–fig. 6.8). However, do keep in mind that

RIGHT ARM STRIKE

FIGURE 6.1 WIDE RIGHT PUNCH—FRONT VIEW

This is what I commonly see from beginners' hand strikes—wide, swinging motions that are clumsy in nature. This is especially true when this type of martial artist is stressed and must react quickly. That's when the cream rises to the top and you can really see what skill level a practitioner has developed. I can tell you this—anyone who implements this sort of motion will certainly deal with some bumps and bruises. As you can see, this method leaves the practitioner quite vulnerable. Remember, the tighter or more refined your movements become, the more efficient you become. It's okay and even expected for a beginner to move with this kind of action. However, once you're more experienced, you have to polish up your movements so they take on the role of a Swiss watch—to display precise physical motion.

FIGURE 6.2 STRAIGHT RIGHT PUNCH—FRONT VIEW

This is a refined technique. This type of striking motion takes time to develop and requires a lot of repetition. Most novice martial arts practitioners look at this type of motion and think it's easy to execute. However, when I pressure them in sparring matches, the quality of their techniques flies out the window, and soon they are just flailing away. The fact of the matter is that if you can't subconsciously perform this type of motion under pressure, then you haven't developed it—or, as I would say, internalized it. It is your normal visceral reaction that counts. If you can't perform it under pressure, then you haven't achieved this type of refined movement.

OUTWARD WRIST LOCK

I want to issue a word of caution here. I don't want you to even attempt this lesson in new motions from my dojo. However, I do want you to pay close attention to what my sparring partner and I are showing you about exaggerated motion.

FIGURE 6.3 OUTWARD WRIST LOCK (WIDE)—SIDE VIEW

The technique I'm using for this example is a common wrist lock. I selected it because it's a little easier for you to visually pick up the wide motions. It is a very effective technique and one that was taught to me early on in my training. What I really want you to zoom in on for this sequence is the wide movements I'm making with my arms while I'm executing the technique. This is how I teach a beginning martial arts student the proper angle and direction necessary to effectively use this maneuver. It is the wide, exaggerated motions that let a student see what I'm doing. On the other hand, if I were to perform this technique at a high level, the student wouldn't be able to see each element of the movement. That's why the principle of new motions is so important—it lets the student identify what type of motion is needed to accomplish a chosen action.

FIGURE 6.4 OUTWARD WRIST LOCK (TIGHT)—SIDE VIEW

Now it's time to look at the real deal. This is how a seasoned martial artist would perform an outward wrist lock. Again, focus in on the movements I'm making with my arms. This time you will notice that they're staying closer to me and not extending as much. That should give you a signal that the circular motion I'm using for this technique is becoming more refined. As a student, it might take you several months of repeating this move over and over to finally perform it at normal speed and truly be able to execute it with a resisting training partner. But once all the precise angles and directions have sunk in, it's yours: it is internalized. You will be able to subconsciously use this movement and not over-analyze its functions. That is your goal, and if you have the determination to keep training, anyone, and I mean anyone, can achieve these results.

this principle can be applied to every physical motion you make in the golf swing. This just happens to be one of the most significant elements in your swing—which is why I selected it.

FIGURE 6.5 SETUP TO TOP OF BACKSWING (WIDE), 6-IRON—FRONT VIEW

To encourage a proper loading of weight on the right side in the backswing, a wide motion, such as what you see here, is prescribed. It gives the student a feel for what loading is really all about. But, as you know by now, a refined motion, shown in the next figure, is the goal.

FIGURE 6.6 Setup to top of backswing (normal), 6-iron—front view

The weight shift has taken place in this sequence; however, it is more abbreviated and not as noticeable. That is the sign of skilled motion. With a trained eye, you could just look at the position of my head in relation to the ball. In the previous backswing, my head was much farther behind the ball—this means that I magnified the motion. The objective, though, is to use the movement from this set.

FIGURE 6.7 DOWNSWING TO JUST PAST IMPACT (WIDE), 6-IRON—FRONT VIEW

The body motion of your downswing is certainly a key factor in making solid contact. If you lack side-to-side (lateral) motion when you're swinging the club down into impact, you may as well close your eyes, because the results aren't worth watching. You must, and I mean *must*, shift to the left in your downswing.

    This sequence demonstrates excessive lateral motion—my body and arms are shifting toward the target with quite a bit of motion. This type of action is useful in conditioning your body for proper response.

FIGURE 6.8 DOWNSWING TO JUST PAST IMPACT (NORMAL), 6-IRON—FRONT VIEW

This sequence gives you the road map for polished movement. You can see that my body weight has shifted onto my left side and my right heel has raised. These are two key elements in detecting lateral motion for the downswing. You can see that a more balanced structure is shown, a connection of the arms, the upper torso, and—the tell-all—correct head positioning.

SUMMARY

New motion principles have turned on your power sources by exaggerating movements, stripping away the unessentials, and narrowing your backswing and downswing to their core. Again, I think one of my master teachers said it best: "The outstanding characteristic of the expert athletes is their ease of movement." That really hit home for me—I hope those words of wisdom hit home for you as well.

It looks like you're ready for the next building block in Balanced Golf—coordination drills and exercises. These Eastern and Western methods will permanently bond relaxed movement and explosive yang into your swing. So, enter through the next doorway of your personal development.

7

THE BEST OF EAST AND WEST—
BODY MOTION AND THE ARM SWING

It's all about yin and yang. You have seen this every step of the way on our Eastern path. Now, prepare for an entirely new way of looking at body motion and the arm swing, the key flow of unforced yin and yang for the golfer. That's you, and now you're ready to blend Western and Eastern coordination drills for perfect balance and perfect power. All of these drills and exercises are simple, but together they will lift your game to a higher level of performance. They will offer you the ideal problem-solving program, because with regular practice you can head off any number of flaws in your swing. Just as important, if you're already wrestling with a specific rotational, rhythm, or arm swing problem, you can combine specific Western and Eastern techniques to cure that problem for good. I have developed and tested all of the drills in this chapter, and I've seen the

difference they make for my students. That difference is a swing that truly combines the best of East and West—a balanced swing for a better, more enjoyable game.

You know where we're headed now. It's back to the practice tee for an expanded look at body motion and the arm swing in the classic Western style.

WESTERN BODY MOTION

As we've discussed, the ideal Western swing relies on body and arm swing motion. Now, we are going to consider the muscle groups that play varying roles in your swing.

A simple physical truth is that the large muscle groups of your body are three times stronger and faster than the smaller ones. You can easily put this truth to a golfing test (fig. 7.1a–fig. 7.1f):

1. Pick up three of your irons.
2. Hold all three with a modified baseball grip, using all ten fingers.
3. Take your normal setup.
4. Swing the clubs into your backswing and then into your finish.

Stop now, and think about what your muscles have just told you about the rotational speed of your swing. The large muscle groups of your back, your shoulders, your arms, and your legs did most of the work not only to generate your rotational speed, but also to maintain your balance. That feeling of your large muscle groups dominating and steadying your swing is proper Western body motion. This doesn't mean that your other muscles, the smaller ones, don't do their part. But you must realize that it's the larger ones that fuel the bulk of your rotational speed and force.

"Force" is the key word here. If you watch a PGA Tour player swing his driver at speeds of 110 MPH or more, you're probably so caught up in how far the ball travels that you've missed something. That

A

D

B

C

E

F

FIGURE 7.1 Setup through finish holding three clubs—front view

"something" is everything to a controlled and powerful body motion and arm swing. In order to maintain satisfactory balance for the swing's power, Tiger Woods, Ernie Els, John Daly, and every other big hitter must allow their body motion to follow the proper laws of movement. Since these great players must comply to these principles, so must you and I. There is no arguing against balanced movement. If Tiger were to let his arms work against his torso, even he would spray shots all over the place. However, as we've all seen, he doesn't let this happen. Neither does any player who wants a consistent, powerful swing.

For a classic swing, your body must be the nucleus of the swing. For example, picture yourself as the center, or the hub, of a circle and your clubhead as the outer line of the circle, its forceful line. Simple physics teaches us that the center of any circle controls the speed of the outer edge. For a golfer, of course, the outer edge is the clubhead.

A simple experiment really illustrates the way in which the circle's hub (the golfer's body) controls the speed of the outer edge (the clubhead). If we were actually standing

together at the practice range, I would now hand you a small plumber's washer tied to a piece of twine. So, I would like you to head to the cellar or garage to make your own weight and string. Hold the unweighted side of the string, and spin the weight at different rates of speed. You will feel that when your hand moves faster or slower, the weight also speeds up or slows down in its path.

How does our little physics project relate to your golf swing? Your spinning hand represents the body motion you generate in your swing. The washer, which represents your clubhead, travels only as fast or as slow as your hand allows. Let's say you begin to spin your hand wildly. The washer will travel in an uncontrollable path. That is exactly what happens if you can't control—synchronize—your body motion and arms in your golf swing. Conversely, if you slow down your spinning hand to a crawl, the washer also loses force. This same slowdown plagues golfers whose synchronization of body and arms is too weak to generate much force. Such players are just as guilty of poor body and arm motion as fast and wild swingers. The key is to find a smooth, strong, and steady tempo that's comfortable for you.

A lack of comfort causes golfers to do some pretty drastic things during the swing, and none of them are good. What are they? Let's break them down into body motion flaws and arm swing flaws. If you're guilty of any of these golf sins, pay close attention as I discuss faulty rotation and erratic arm swing paths. You will recognize your particular problem and, as you will soon learn, that's half of the solution for Balanced Golf.

Common Body Motion Flaws

As you know, your golfing body has two key elements, the upper torso and the lower body. It is vital that they work in unison. Your upper torso must maintain a position that's directly above your lower body. If your position is even slightly off, you're creating additional body angles. Your off-kilter alignments require your body to compensate for the error: they force you to use more motion than you should in your swing. That's because these unwanted actions are the only

hope you have to regain proper positions. It's simply too much work for any player.

How much work are we talking about here? Think of it this way: every unnecessary and unwanted motion you add to your swing means another component to your swing. And the hard fact is that it takes a lot of practice and determination just to control the swing's necessary components. So, what you have to do is adopt the mentality of a sculptor and chip away all of the unessential and harmful pieces of your swing.

Let's examine the pieces that have to go.

Incorrect Body Weighting in the Backswing

If your upper body tilts to the left at the top of your backswing, you create a reverse weight shift (fig. 7.2). This is an abnormal transfer of body weight onto your left side, and this tilt is so harmful that it hurts not only your backswing, but also your downswing. Remember the words, "for every action, there is a reaction."

Ideally, you want your body weight to move from a centered position at the start to the inside of

FIGURE 7.2 TOP OF BACKSWING (REVERSE WEIGHT SHIFT), DRIVER—FRONT VIEW

FIGURE 7.3 TOP OF BACKSWING (UPPER BODY LEANING RIGHT), DRIVER—FRONT VIEW

your right leg during the backswing. If you tilt to the left in your setup or anywhere in your backswing, a large portion of your body weight is going to stay there. Your posture and your swing are unbalanced before your clubhead is anywhere near the ball. There is no way you can undo that sort of imbalance before impact.

With this leftward tilt, you're primed for part two—the reaction—of your improper weight shift. In your downswing, the faulty reaction is that too much of your

weight moves to your right side. This condition defeats any chance that you'll have 80 percent of your weight on your left leg in the finish. Upper-body tilt is a part you have to chip away from your swing. Otherwise, you can't properly move your body weight from your back, or support, leg to the forward leg.

Now, let's examine what happens if you forsake your upper torso and lower body alignments for a tilt to the right (fig. 7.3). You're going to have a terrible time making solid contact: you have shifted your weight beyond the outside of your right leg. Simply put, you have too much distance to recover in the downswing. There just isn't any way you can move your weight back to the left quickly enough. The result? You don't have full power, the added weight you need for proper distance, at impact.

Upper Torso Tilt in the Downswing

You wouldn't believe how many golfers come to me with a problem whose "rightness" is absolutely wrong. I am talking about players whose upper torso leans back to the right as their club reaches impact (fig. 7.4). This right-sided tilt is a blueprint for erratic shots: you will squander upper torso strength and likely create too much hand activity at impact. Because this lean gets your hands moving in all directions, your club will descend into the ball with a poor angle. Slices, hooks, topped shots, pop-ups—you'll hit them all if you're always leaning back to the right at impact.

If you are someone who takes the opposite tilt, to the left, in the downswing, you are equally susceptible to erratic shots. An upper torso tilted to the left during the

FIGURE 7.4 IMPACT (UPPER BODY LEANING RIGHT), DRIVER—FRONT VIEW

downswing prevents a smooth, synchronized motion because your arms and hands are doing too much work (fig. 7.5). They are trying to compensate for the excessive weight that's anchored on your left side, rather than moving through impact. This condition creates a miserable angle of attack. I have found that students who come to me with this leftward leaning action tend to activate their forearms and hands way too much. The outcome? The dreaded hook shot again and again.

FIGURE 7.5 IMPACT (UPPER BODY LEANING LEFT), DRIVER—FRONT VIEW

again, remember that for a balanced, strong motion, you can move your head a few inches to the right in the backswing and twice that distance to the left in the downswing. Don't hold on to rigid notions of a locked head! This is truly a habit you must change if you want dynamic motion in your swing.

The Western Arm Swing

Ideal body motion (fig. 7.6 and 7.7) depends to a great extent on the correct arm swing. The arm swing, in turn, depends on several factors: your hands, arms, and upper torso; the speed and path of your swing; and your target line.

Hands

If, at the setup, your hands are positioned lower than what's natural or comfortable for you, you will increase your hand activity in both the backswing and the downswing. You don't want your hands to take over; you do want them to perform their key task—to hinge the club in a gradual motion while your body and arms, not your hands, do most of the work. It's your arms that have to create a long, wide arc with the club.

Head Movement

In discussing body motion, I must come back to something we've discussed in previous chapters, something that a few of my PGA colleagues have a bit of difficulty accepting. Maybe you've guessed where I'm going here—to the very top, the head. The Balanced Golf techniques you have learned emphasize fluid, dynamic movement. That means you don't freeze your head during the golf swing. So, once

THE IDEAL WESTERN BODY MOTION

FIGURE 7.6 TOP OF BACKSWING (CORRECT), DRIVER—FRONT VIEW

In the classic Western backswing, the upper torso is vertical from the belt line to the top of the head. This position aligns you for a proper downswing. Here, again, you use your left shoulder as a reference point. It should be slightly behind the ball.

FIGURE 7.7 IMPACT (CORRECT), DRIVER—FRONT VIEW

At the ideal impact position, it is a given that both your lower body and upper torso move together. Your weight shifts smoothly to the left side, and your arms move through impact with no self-imposed obstacles. These are the Western cornerstones of a repeatable swing.

Because your hands are your actual connection to the club, you might have a hard time making your hands surrender most of the swing's work to your arms and body. For instance, some of my students who play racquetball—where the game's speed produces a lot of shots that depend on the hands and wrists—come to me with particular trouble in calming down their hands on the golf club. I first explain to them that the same hand action that creates some terrific kill shots in racquetball creates havoc in a golf swing. Overly active hands in the golf swing mean that a player must time his or her arms and body in unison with extra hand activity. I can tell you firsthand that there aren't many players who can do that on a consistent basis. Even worse, extra hand action produces inconsistent angles of attack for the clubhead. That translates into every bad shot known and follows with bogey after bogey.

When I talk about you becoming a golf sculptor, chipping away unwanted extra parts from your swing, hand motions that excessively twist or hinge the club are parts that have to go. Once your grip is comfortably in place, you have sent a message to your hands—stay firm, stay supple, and don't twist the club beyond reason.

Position and Path

The ideal position for your arms is at a slight angle away from your body. This angle sets your arms on the plane, or better yet the path, that they will follow throughout your swing. Basically, the plane is your predetermined arm swing path.

However, if your arms are positioned too vertical to the ground and don't create a slight angle, you will produce an extra and unwelcome part in your swing, two motions for the price of one. What's

the fee? It's a linear—straightback—arm swing that certainly doesn't lead to straight shots. That's because when your arms are set in this vertical position, they tend to move in a linear motion as opposed to a circular one. As the club moves in this linear path, you must struggle to adjust it back into its proper position. Here is where you force your hands to become overly active and your wrists hinge the club too quickly. Even if the club is back on a circular plane, the angle of attack is altered and a slice or hook is waiting in the wings.

The Western solution is to allow your arms to move in a circular motion by positioning them slightly away from your body.

Speed

I'm sure a golf instructor has told you that moving the club in the correct path is crucial to a solid swing. I agree with that statement and emphasize it to all my students. So, now come the questions: how fast should your arms travel going back and coming down; and how fast should your body rotate? I will address both of these questions in a moment. First, however, I want you to remember an undeniable relationship between your swing's arm speed and your body rotation: when either one is increased, your swing path can take a detour and force the club to take on a whole new position. The fact is that whether your swing speed hits 90 MPH or 110 MPH, your arm swing and body rotation must work in unison.

I have spent many hours consulting with some of the game's top players about the vital role of arm speed in their swing. All of them, from Seve Ballesteros to Brad Faxon to Ray Floyd, agree that your arms should not accelerate until your left arm is parallel to the ground in your downswing. At this point, the club should be moving on the proper path and plane. In theory, my colleagues and I all agree that in the swing's motion, only one point of maximum speed exists. That point is impact.

Now, let's talk about what your maximum speed should be at impact. The *simple* truth is that there's a different comfort level for speed in each golfer's swing. The *hard* truth is that the incredible clubhead speed generated by Tour greats is beyond the coordination level of most weekend players. That

is because the professionals' natural ability and a lifetime of practice has allowed them to time their arm swing speed and body rotation in perfect harmony. Average and even talented amateurs shouldn't take that reality too hard, however, because they can achieve maximum speed to launch long, solid shots as well.

I have envisioned the speed of a swing by comparing it to the tachometer in an automobile. A car's motor has its own comfort level for operation, say 1,000 to 6,000 RPMs. If a driver pushes the engine's speed beyond its proper level, the engine becomes stressed and a mechanical failure follows. It's the same with your golf swing. First, you need to learn just how fast you can swing the club comfortably—I strongly suggest that you do this with a qualified golf instructor. Second, you should be aware of your top speed and then cut it back to 80 percent. This is an area on which I specifically spend lots of time with my students. I make sure that they are aware of their maximum speed and tell them we're not going to floor their swing at that speed—we're going to set it for 80 percent power.

As you can guess, at first some of my pupils, especially men, resist me a little on the swing speed issue. "Why can't I air it out now that I've found my top speed?" they ask. I answer that I am going to give them a "safety switch" to guarantee that they won't stress out their swing by running it at its maximum RPM every time. The switch cuts a player back to 80 percent, which assures them of a well-balanced swing. It's simply too much for most players to swing as fast as possible every time.

Sometimes, swing speed diehards need an example from the Tour. My favorite is the one I've presented before—Davis Love III. Remember how he gave up a little distance for a repeatable swing? If a player of his stature can adjust, so can you. And running your swing at 80 percent of its full speed is the way to go for a balanced swing.

So, what does 80 percent feel like? It feels different for each golfer. Strength, height, physical condition, and every conceivable physical trait all differ in every player. This is why you have to head to the driving range and hit a lot of practice shots. You have to determine how fast you can swing the club and still control it. This isn't the same thing as swinging hard, which is forcing the club and ruining any hope of a balanced swing. Basically, you have to let the club do its job by swinging smoothly and keeping your stance balanced. If you're swinging too hard, you will feel strain in your upper torso, your arms, your hips—just about everywhere. Worst of all, the club will be off course coming into the ball. But when you feel the club and your body working in unison, you will know that your personal speedometer, and that of the club, are in sync.

The Target Line

There is a useful tool to monitor the direction of your arm swing path. It's the target line. Your downswing can take three basic paths, but only one is correct.

• Inside and down the target line (fig. 7.8a–fig. 7.8d). This is the ideal path for the club and your arms to follow. By promoting this type of action, you will minimize the curving flight of your shots—whether they are slices or hooks.

• Inside to outside (fig. 7.9a–fig. 7.9d). This is without a doubt the most common flaw in arm swing paths. If you are a golfer with this

A

B

C

D

Figure 7.8 Setup through downswing (correct), 6-iron—side view

A   B

C   D

FIGURE 7.9 SETUP THROUGH DOWNSWING (INSIDE TO OUTSIDE), 6-IRON—SIDE VIEW

kind of motion, you try to make a deep turn in the backswing, sometimes overdoing it, and follow it up with a twisting motion in the downswing. The problem with this scenario is that it causes extreme positions. The club gets yanked inside going back, and then your body responds by sending it out and away from you in the downswing. This creates a wide array of shots that mostly pull to the left, in either a slice or a hook. Remember, for every action you create a reaction.

• Outside to inside (fig. 7.10a– fig. 7.10d). This is another fairly common arm swing problem. In this situation, a golfer usually attempts to move the club straight back in the backswing. However, once the downswing begins, he or she tends to twist the body quickly, and this causes the club and arms to move over the target line, well out to the right. Most of the time this type of player will produce severe hooking shots. The initial ball flight starts out to the right of the intended target but then hooks back—sometimes more, sometimes less. It creates an unpredictable situation, and certainly one that no golfer should be required to manage.

The point to remember about swing path is that for every action you produce a reaction. Any excessive positions will promote significant problems for you. In addition, by matching your backswing and downswing paths, you minimize your hand and forearm rotation during the swing. That means you're going to hit straighter shots, and we all know that's a good thing!

I'm sure you have noticed how Tour players hit their shots straight most of the time. Whether they're hitting a fade or a draw, their shots fly straight for the most part. However, once the shots rise to their apex—the highest point—they curve in one direction or the other on the way down. So, for highly skilled players and amateurs alike, the less curvature produced with the ball, the better. And the best part is that more shots will land on the fairway or the green.

Arms and Upper Torso
Our last Western word on the swing's classic connection between body motion and the arm swing is the link between your arms and your upper torso. I'll bet you've read a lot about connection in golf magazines in recent years. Unfortunately, you

A

B

C

D

FIGURE 7.10 SETUP THROUGH DOWNSWING (OUTSIDE TO INSIDE), 6-IRON—SIDE VIEW

might be one of the many players I've found who take one part of this connection theory to the extreme. The part I'm referring to is the one that insists you keep both of your arms close to your upper torso as you swing. Close is correct, but many players have literally gotten their arms too close for comfort.

How do you know if you're one of these players? For openers, if you practice either of the following drills, you probably are:

- Wrap a large bath towel around your upper body and under your arms while you practice your swing.
- You have purchased one of those elastic-band devices that wrap around your upper torso and restrain your arms as you swing the club.

There are many more drills and devices like these. I steer my students away from them as quickly as possible. Before Western purists accuse me of disagreeing with the arm–body connection, let me assure you that I'm only taking issue with any Western technique that restrains both arms or, especially, restricts fluid movement of the left arm. Again, although other instructors may disagree, I would toss away any aids or drills that limit the movement of your left arm. They simply encourage rigidity and can ruin a swing.

Now, let's shift to the connection of your right arm to your upper torso during the swing. Your right arm's humerus (bone), stretching from your elbow to your shoulder, is the most important connection to your torso during the swing. As long as you maintain this connection, your arms will stay relatively close to you and have an easy time matching the movements of your body.

Once in a great while, I have come across students who swing with a "flying right elbow." This condition pops up when their right arm moves an excessive distance from their body. Jack Nicklaus and Miller Barber have followed their flying right elbows to Hall of Fame careers. Although few flying elbow players will ever match Jack's and Miller's results, some fine golfers do possess enough coordination to swing with this sort of positioning and still keep their shots on target. If you happen to be one of these players, I'll give you the same advice

I give my students: let your elbow fly until or unless you begin to spray shots all over the course.

For most—actually, almost all—players, the less their right elbow flies away from their upper torso, the better their swing. To illustrate this truth, a look at figure skating is helpful. When a world-class skater begins any stationary spiraling movement, they extend their arms out to the side at shoulder level. Once they move into the actual circular (spinning) motion and need to increase rotational speed, they bring their arms closer to their body. For the golfer, these alignments demonstrate two key points:

- Your body can increase its rotational speed when your arms are *connected* to your body.
- In order to maintain proper posture and balance, most golfers let their arms fly away from their upper torso.

At this point, you're probably anticipating your next Eastern lesson, the means to balance your Western body motion and arm swing. I have a little surprise: we're going to do something a bit different. First we are going to perform a series of Western coordination drills that we will blend with Eastern techniques for the ultimate balance and power in your swing. This is the point where the best of East and West will truly meet and revolutionize your game for good. This is also where I will reveal Balanced Golf's powerful yet simple guideposts for permanent problem solving in your swing. It almost sounds too good to be true—but it is true. You are approaching the crossroads where traditional Western drills and the techniques of the dojo truly become one route.

YOUR WESTERN COORDINATES

When students come to me with specific swing problems, I show them one or two Western coordination drills that counter these flaws. By "counter," I'm talking about methods that provide the opposite result to a nagging error. This opposing action allows a student to find the middle ground between two extremes. Between a slice and a hook lies a straight shot—the middle ground. What these drills do is recoordinate a swing flaw so that you can recondition your natural response.

Perhaps you have tackled swing problems by turning to drills or teaching aids that seek to calm your swing by restricting it. You already know my aversion to gadgets that confine your swing, and my feeling about nonrealistic drills isn't much different. I firmly advocate the opposite approach—almost all of the drills I recommended are dynamic, like a real swing. Dynamic drills simulate actual ball striking, actual club movements. For every one of my drills, you'll need a ball, because I want you to hit shots. Even if you're not at the driving range, you can perform these drills with whiffle or soft-foam practice balls in your backyard or even off a practice mat in your garage. So, there's no excuse for resisting dynamic drills in favor of gadgets and swing-pantomime practice sessions.

A hundred or more repetitions with some gadget on your wrist, your waist, your arms, or your legs don't—in my opinion and experience—do much for you when you unhook or unstrap the device and take real swings that don't even resemble a proper one. Of course, a handful of swing aids have their uses, but overall the majority of these "cure-alls" only relieve the manufacturers' cash flow. Most gimmicks and gadgets won't lower your scores, but they will empty your pocket. One last warning here: you can't buy a swing; you have to build one. The upcoming Western and Eastern coordination drills are your building blocks for a balanced, repeatable swing.

The only "devices" you need for the Western drills are in your golf bag. I will start you off with a 6-iron because it's the perfect tool for your swing's middle ground, a medium-length club that gives you the basic feel of both short and long shots. Once you're comfortable with your 6-iron, you can use any wood or iron in your bag.

Before you grab your club, I have to throw another adage at you. You know the expression "you have to walk before you can run." It applies to the drills I'm about to show you. Your key to maximum results from these exercises is to perform them slowly and allow your arms to flow with a comfortable action. A slow arm swing will provide you with the time to feel and fix a mechanical problem.

For those of you who "feel the need for speed" even in practice, let me tell you why you have to slow down if you want the drills to help you. Let's say that your idea of a good practice session is to bang around a hundred or so balls at full speed (6-iron shots average 85 to 90 MPH). Assuming that you've hit fifty of them straight, you're still spraying half of your shots around. You're doing something wrong, and, believe me, I'm being generous in assuming most golfers hit half of those balls solidly.

The thing we have to do now is to identify what you're doing wrong with your all-out swing. First of all, your club's moving too fast for you to narrow down what's good and what's bad about your swing. That's bad practice—quantity over quality. So, I'm going to ask you to slow down your swing speed by at least a third when you practice the drills. Again, don't worry about some internal speedometer. Think of the process as slowing down from a run to a jog, or a jog to a walk.

Remember that I'm not asking you to downshift your swing speed permanently, only as you practice the drills. Then, when you've mas-

tered the motions, you can turn on the juice where it really counts—on the course. On the practice tee and in the dojo, you can speed up any physical motion once you've grasped every bit of that movement at a beginner's pace.

Now, pick up that 6-iron, and let's get started on your Western coordination drills.

Drills for Proper Body Motion

Half-to-Half Drill
I use this drill for students suffering from poor body motion and ineffective weight shifts.

1. Take your normal stance (fig. 7.11a).
2. Swing your 6-iron back about halfway; you can hinge your wrists slightly (fig. 7.11b). Because you're swinging at a reduced speed, you'll feel your head moving slightly. Let that happen! If you fight it, rigidity will creep in.
3. Move from your transition to your downswing (fig. 7.11c). Now, because you've slowed down your movements, you will

A   B   C

D   E   F

FIGURE 7.11   HALF-TO-HALF DRILL, 6-IRON—FRONT VIEW

really feel your weight—your entire body—shift to the left. And because you're using a slower pace with your arms, your body rotation will decrease automatically.

4. As you move slowly into impact, you have time to check whether your body's center is where it should be: in line with or slightly ahead of the ball (fig. 7.11d–fig. 7.11e). Either position guarantees a proper striking angle at impact.

   Because of your reduced rotational speed throughout the drill, you'll find it's easier to time your arms in unison with your body. When you hit real shots on the course, you'll be able to coordinate your arms and body at an optimum speed because your slower practices have instinctively groomed you for the same movements at a higher speed.

5. In your final position, your entire body should be vertical, no leaning back on the right leg (fig. 7.11f). You should have shifted most of your weight to the left leg.

Remember that the Half-to-Half Drill is a miniswing, but it contains all of the full swing's necessary elements of fluid body motion and smooth weight shifts.

Left-Foot Shuffle

No, this isn't a dance step. The Left-Foot Shuffle is a proven method for developing proper body motion in your swing, and it also helps any golfer who has a hard time with weight shifts during the swing.

Two other reasons that I like this drill so much are that it gives you instant feedback if your body motion is off, and that it reinforces a correct, stacked body position for your upper torso and lower body. So, grab your 6-iron again, and get ready to shuffle.

1. Set up over the ball (fig. 7.12a).
2. As you take your backswing, slide your left foot next to your right (fig. 7.12b–fig. 7.12c). The move will feel awkward at first, but will get better after several repetitions.
3. Continue swinging the club back to a three-quarter backswing.
4. As you move from your transition to your downswing, slide your left foot back to its original position (fig. 7.12d–fig. 7.12e).

A

B

C

D

E

F

G

FIGURE 7.12 LEFT-FOOT SHUFFLE, 6-IRON—FRONT VIEW

5. Move through impact and into your normal finish (fig. 7.12f–fig. 7.12g). Your end position should mirror that for any solid shot: your weight on your left side, your body position straight, and you are rotated onto your right toe.

The Left-Foot Shuffle is a terrific drill for anyone whose arms take over the swing. The reason the shuffle is so effective is that it teaches an arms-only player how to add all-important lateral motion to his or her swing.

Body Rotation Drills

One-Foot Drill

Here is an ideal drill for golfers plagued by excessive body rotation. This routine emphasizes your arm swing by reducing body activity.

1. Take your normal setup (fig. 7.13a).
2. Pull back your right foot so the heel of your left foot and the toes of your right foot are next to each other (fig. 7.13b). Make sure that you space your feet only three to six inches apart. Keep your knees flexed.

3. Swing the club slowly into your backswing, using a reduced length (fig. 7.13c–fig. 7.13d).

4. As you move into your down-swing and finish, your club should end up near your left shoulder (fig. 7.13e–fig. 7.13g).

So, what have you experienced from setup to finish in this drill? You should have felt your arms dominate your swing and your body rotation limited. By offsetting your excessive body rotation, you're allowing your arms to do most of the work.

A

D

E

B

C

F

G

FIGURE 7.13 One-Foot Drill, 6-iron—front view

By practicing this exercise, you'll find that whenever you take your normal swing, your arms will work with your body. You counter the excess rotation through the extreme arm swing of the One-Foot Drill. Now, you can find the appropriate middle ground that allows you to blend your arm swing and body rotation for a unified swing. With just a few one-foot swings, you'll find that your lower body action slows down and your timing improves.

Crossing Arms Drill

This one is another dynamic Western drill tailored for golfers with excessive body rotation. The routine is also terrific for players who are simply striving to integrate a better arm swing and body-turn sequence.

1. Take a wider than normal setup, and flex your knees more than usual (fig. 7.14a). The increased knee flex acts as a "lock down" for your body, preventing it from moving up, down, left, or right.
2. Using a slow arm speed, take a short swing, back and through, but don't let your body rotate (fig. 7.14b–fig. 7.14g). That's

right—no rotation at all. Throughout your backswing, downswing, and finish, your entire body should face the ball (target line). This position will feel really uncomfortable, but it won't put undue stress on your body.

You have to be patient with this drill because it's awkward enough that some players think they must be doing it wrong. If you stick with this drill, it will teach you to control your rotation by countering one extreme motion with the opposite extreme. With practice, you'll find that middle point between too much and too little rotation.

I have used the Crossing Arms Drill with many students who had no concept of proper body motion. They would simply step up to the ball, twist and turn through their swing, and feel miserable as their shots turned up everywhere except on a fairway or a green. For these golfers, Crossing Arms was a real eye-opener. When they got to their finish in the drill, they were startled that their hips and upper torso faced the target. But, with continual practice, they achieved proper body rotation courtesy of Crossing Arms.

FIGURE 7.14 CROSSING ARMS DRILL, 6-IRON—
FRONT VIEW

Arm Swing Drills

Long and Slow Drill

For players whose swings are too
fast, disrupting proper unison
between their arms and body, or
players who struggle with a smooth
transition, the Long and Slow Drill
is a perfect solution. This drill can
even help a golfer who has a short,
constricted backswing and needs to
lengthen it.

Before we begin the exercise, I
would like you to put your 6-iron
back in the bag and take out your
sand wedge, your 5-iron, and your
driver. That's right, even your driver,
the longest club you own. With
these three clubs, which cover all
the major ranges of length and loft,
I'm going to show you how the
Long and Slow exercise can help
you build an arsenal of smooth and
accurate shots.

We will start with the smallest
of your three weapons—the sand
wedge. It's a great way to begin
because a well-hit lob, or flop shot,
can save you a lot of strokes. How
many times have you seen "escape
artist" Seve Ballesteros carry tough
flop shots over a water hazard, a
sand bunker, or a mound and nail a
birdie? In your own foursomes, I bet

the player who has the sharpest
touch with a sand wedge or a lob
wedge often cards the lowest score.
Let's get you headed in that direction. In fact, you are about to learn
that the flop can make the rest of
your game a hit.

You probably know how a flop
is supposed to be hit, but let's
review it just in case:

1. Use your usual sand wedge
   setup, keeping the ball position
   forward, toward your left foot.
2. Take a full-length swing with
   substantially reduced speed (fig.
   7.15a–fig. 7.15e). Your ball
   should fly high and land softly
   without rolling too much.
3. Hit twenty flops in a row. Take
   your time!

As soon as you feel comfortable
swinging the wedge, put it back in
the bag and pick up your 5-iron.
You are going to use the same long
and slow method here:

1. Take your normal setup.
2. Hit twenty balls with your normal stance and swing length,
   but swing with the same
   reduced speed you used for the
   flop shot (fig. 7.16a–fig. 7.16e).

A

B

C

D

E

FIGURE 7.15 Long and Slow Drill (flop shot), sand wedge—front view

A

B

C

D

E

FIGURE 7.16 LONG AND SLOW DRILL, 5-IRON—FRONT VIEW

Now that you fast swingers out there have heard the message of long and slow, it's time to reach for the club that makes just about everyone feel like swinging hard and fast. Great Big Bertha, Fat Shaft, Titleist Titanium—whichever driver you reach for doesn't matter in this drill, because you are going to file away that swing-from-the-heels mentality and swing that big club long and slow.

1. Set up in your normal stance. Don't do anything different in your address.

2. Take a full swing—takeaway to finish—but hit the ball using the flop shot mode of thought, long and slow (fig. 7.17a–fig. 7.17c).

3. Hit twenty balls using this method.

What can regular practice of this trio of flop shots—wedge, 5-iron, and driver—do for a golfer whose swing is too fast and can't be controlled? By swinging a long club, a medium club, and a short club long and slow in practice, you make the simple concept of slowing down

A

B

C

FIGURE 7.17 LONG AND SLOW DRILL, DRIVER—FRONT VIEW

your swing not just a mental key, but a muscle memory. When you swing that oversized driver in a round, you won't, of course, slow down your tempo to flop shot speed. You will, however, tone down your swing speed enough to control it, because the three-club drill has taught you how to "brake" your swing just enough to manage it. Best of all, results won't take long if you practice Long and Slow. As a matter of fact, those three words are a pretty good mantra.

Club the Ball Drill

Okay, I have a gimmick in this drill. But the gimmick is one that's acceptable to even the most traditional players. After all, what's more traditional than the golf ball itself?

Most importantly, the drill I have named Club the Ball can help golfers tormented by poor arm swing and club-path direction. You can use any club except your putter in this routine, but if you are struggling with a particular club, that's the one I want you to use. This drill can restore or enhance your "club confidence," so if you feel insecure about a certain club, choose it and change your confidence level right now.

1. Take your setup over the ball and choose a target (fig. 7.18a). Once your target is selected, you have also determined your target line—the imaginary line along which the ball should travel.
2. Place a second ball fifteen to twenty inches behind the first ball, and move the second ball off the target line and toward you three to four inches.
3. Take your normal swing, but use the second ball as your visual reference—you are trying to move the club over it (fig. 7.18b–fig. 7.18d). By doing so, you can establish a proper path for the club in your backswing.
4. Continue through impact and into your finish (fig. 7.18e–fig. 7.18f).

During this exercise, your peripheral vision will spot the second ball and, despite the distraction, you will have a great reference point for your club path. Your goal is to move the clubhead over the second ball in your backswing and then do the same as your downswing heads toward impact.

Figure 7.18 Club the Ball Drill, 6-iron—side view

Even if you accidentally graze the second ball with your clubhead, don't get discouraged. Keep at it, because that ball is an excellent navigational tool—it helps you form a sound takeaway and steadies your arm swing and club path by making you swing over a fixed point. Diligent practice of Club the Ball will send you into a round with a firm feel of how the club should move around your body and will create a wider arc for more power, a lot more power.

If you have some yellow or orange balls hanging around the garage and thought you would never use them, here's the perfect time. Their bright color makes it easier for you to see them in your peripheral vision and can result in an even better grasp of this exercise.

Hand Lag Drill

If you're a good racquetball or tennis player, you probably improvise a lot of "wristy" shots because of the game's pace. But, as I've mentioned, excessive wrist and hand action in the golf swing doesn't make for winning shots—only shots that fly all over the course.

Whether a player pulls the club inside too quickly or hinges the club upward too steeply, my Hand Lag technique counters both problems equally well. You can practice the drill with any club, but you will achieve your best results by using three to four different clubs during a practice session. That way you can cover various distances.

1. Set up as usual.
2. Move your hands three to five inches into your backswing (fig. 7.19a). That's right—move the grip end of your club first. Make sure the clubhead rests on the ground when you first move your hands. This is your lag position.
3. Move from your lag into the rest of your usual backswing (fig. 7.19b–fig. 7.19c).
4. Continue into your downswing, and go all the way to your finish (fig. 7.19d–fig. 7.19e).

Focus on the drill's second step, the lag position. This position puts your hands in a passive mode before your takeaway even begins. Your hands can bring the club calmly into your backswing. This means

A

B

C

D

E

Figure 7.19 Hand Lag Drill, 6-iron—front view

that you won't pull the club inside too quickly or hinge the club upward too fast. That alone gives you an excellent chance at proper club positioning. Remember, a little lag in your practice sessions will lead to lower rounds.

For those of you who have recognized a personal swing flaw that the Western drills can help offset, I urge you to practice the appropriate exercises. Even though you may not suffer from all of the problems I've covered in these coordination drills, you may be aware of one or more problem areas that could be improved by using them. I guarantee they will reinforce your understanding of proper body and arm swing motion.

Now, I want you to prepare for one of Balanced Golf's most revolutionary approaches: an exercise and coordination program of basic Eastern techniques that are powerful allies to the Western coordination drills. Together, regular practice of both programs will carry your game to its highest level. That's what this blend of East and West has done for me and hundreds of my students. Again, let me assure you that the Asian techniques

involve neither difficult moves nor heavy lifting on your part. If you are willing to practice these Eastern routines, their simplicity will surely revolutionize your game.

EASTERN COORDINATION AND EXERCISE PROGRAM

For a martial artist, training the tools of movement is mandatory. Whether I'm working in a Chinese, Japanese, Korean, or any other martial arts system, I stress that all the steps of a given technique must be in place before a student tries to execute it. That's the only way effective and repeatable motion is possible. Your muscles must be programmed in advance for powerful, balanced movement.

As we return to the dojo, I must tell you that the Eastern drills and exercises you are about to learn are sophisticated in nature but easy to perform. They target all your needs for proper body motion, body rotation, arm swing path, and hand activity. These exercises offer you a way to develop every physical tool you need for a golf swing that moves as it should—with maximum and unforced yin and yang all the way through.

The Eastern exercise program I have developed is important to the performance of your swing because it replaces static positions with dynamic motion. And the simple truth, which is hard for some traditional golf teachers to accept, is that static positions aren't conducive to training your muscles for the necessary motion—the yin and yang—of your swing.

My Eastern exercise and coordination program has three major tools:

- Correct posture
- Stationary exercises
- Moving exercises

There is actually a fourth step, but you are already practicing it: your ki breathing techniques. So, before you begin your Eastern journey to total unison of body and arm motion, I'd like you to reestablish your connection to your one-point. Focus on your lower abdominal area and breathe in and out deeply.

Now that you have your internal ki relaxed and flowing, your one-point is activated. You are ready for the dojo's basic exercises.

Correct Posture

This sounds so basic, almost like when your parents and your teachers told you not to slouch, to sit up straight, or to keep your head up. But, for both the martial artist and the golfer, proper posture doesn't just look good. It is a tool that primes smooth and explosive movement. For the golfer, there's a big difference between what your parents told you and what I'm going to tell you about correct posture. They wanted your head and body straight up. I want you to get everything headed down—grounded.

How do you establish the correct posture? The steps are simple:

1. Stack your upper torso and your lower body with your spine erect and your head level (fig. 7.20).
2. Reestablish your one-point if you feel tightness anywhere in your body.
3. With your arms hanging loosely and your other joints relaxed, let your body weight pull downward—you'll know it's right when you feel that slight heaviness in your arms, shoulders, torso, legs, and feet (fig. 7.21).

FIGURE 7.20 STANDING POSTURE—FRONT VIEW

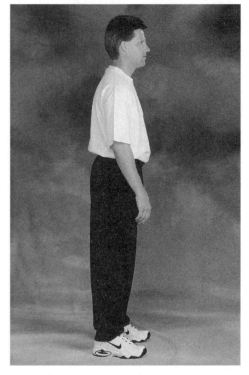

FIGURE 7.21 STANDING POSTURE—SIDE VIEW

As you know, this is grounding, setting your stance to guide the forceful motion of yang. What this simple correct posture technique does for you is to teach you to relax on the mat or on the tee—anytime.

Some of the more common posture errors I see are:

- Shoulders that are tense and shrugging upward
- One shoulder positioned higher than the other

- A tilted head position—too far up, down, or sideways
- One knee bent more than the other

Any or all of these misalignments can cause structural problems. Be sure that you don't fall into one of those traps. I recommend you practice getting into your correct posture and look in the mirror. This gives you a perfect visual reference for checking yourself.

Stationary Exercises

There's that word again—stationary. In the dojo, it doesn't mean standing still. It does mean that your feet aren't moving, but your arms and/or body and head are.

Arm Swinging

Our first stationary exercise is Arm Swinging, a tremendous technique to develop sensitivity to your body rotation and its relationship with your arms.

1. Begin in a normal standing posture, with your limbs relaxed and naturally pulling downward, just like in the Correct Posture method (fig. 7.22a).
2. Turn your body smoothly to the right, allowing your arms to swing freely (fig. 7.22b–fig. 7.22d). Don't jerk your body.
3. Follow by turning smoothly to the left; again, allow your arms to move without restriction (fig. 7.22e–fig. 7.22h).

Have you noticed what your head does as you turn? It rotates with your body in both directions. Your head must move during this exercise, and one reason this is so important to the golfer is that it reinforces the truth that your head must move slightly when you're swinging the club and rotating your body. Arm Swinging trains you to not lock up your head—either during the yin of your setup and transition or the yang of your backswing, downswing, impact, and finish.

As if this isn't good enough, the exercise is also refining three other tools for your balanced swing:

• It relaxes your upper torso and your arms for a smooth swing.
• Your arms respond to your body's turning motion by working in unison with it.
• Because your body weight doesn't shift from side to side (that's the stationary part of this exercise), you isolate the movement of your arms and the turn of your body. This allows your arms and body to remember to work in unison even when you do shift weight in your swing. In other words, Arm Swinging trains your arms to move in coordination with your body turn. Then, once you integrate weight transfer in your swing, it's already a conditioned response.

When you start to practice Arm Swinging, I want you to do it slowly

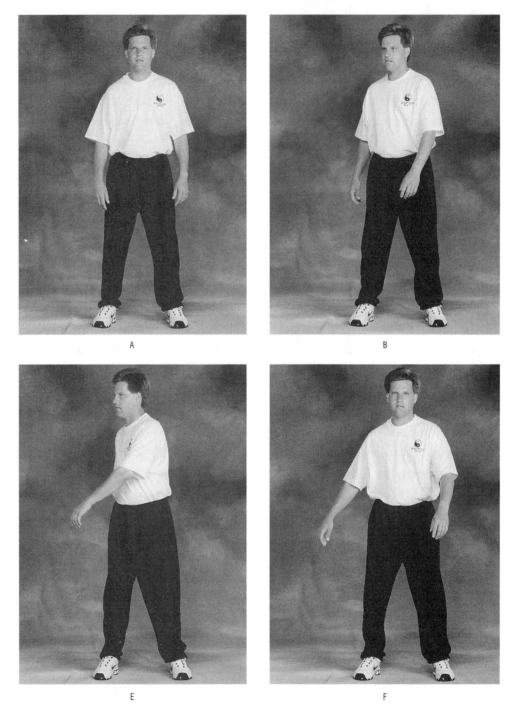

A   B

E   F

FIGURE 7.22 ARM SWINGING—FRONT VIEW

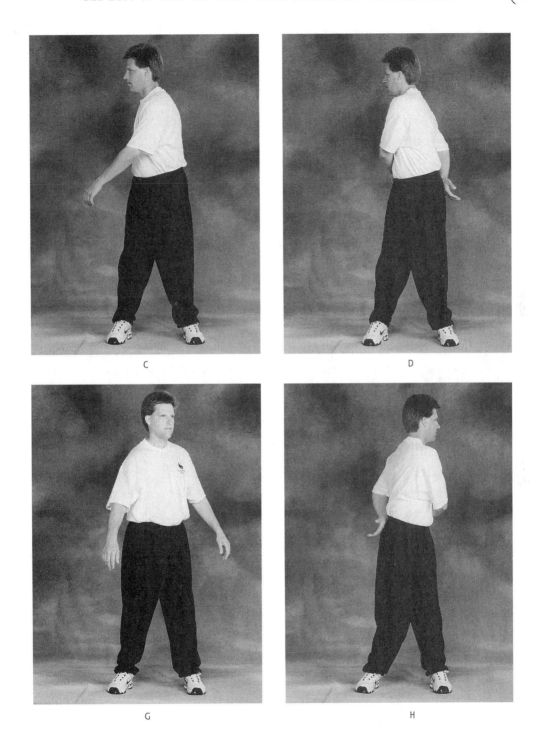

C

D

G

H

and smoothly. Then, as you become more comfortable with the exercise, experiment a little—vary the speed of your turn. You will discover that the faster you turn, the more your arms "fly away" from your body; the slower you turn, the closer your arms stay to your body. This teaches you an important element in your swing: your center controls the power in your swing. And your center is your body. So, if you have a trained and controllable body, you can gauge how much power and speed need to be used for any given shot. That's a pretty significant feather in your golf cap.

As I noted before, you want to swing at about 80 percent of your top speed. By identifying how fast you can swing your arms in this exercise without losing control of them, you have the perfect tool to figure out how fast your 80 percent feels.

Heel Bounce

Our second stationary exercise from the dojo further trains you, the golfer, to maintain a relaxed posture and to feel the essential sensation of your body weight being pulled downward—grounded for balance and fluid motion.

1. Begin in a normal standing posture (fig. 7.23a).
2. Lift both heels off the ground approximately four inches (fig. 7.23b). If, for any reason, you have a problem with four inches, just lift your heels as much as you comfortably can.
3. Slowly ease your heels down. They should touch the ground softly, with minimal contact.
4. Lift your heels back to the four-inch height, or the height you can comfortably reach. Lower back to the ground.
5. Raise and lower your heels in a rhythmic manner. It is a good idea to count as follows: one, raise; two, drop; one, raise; two, drop; and so on. Go through this routine at least twenty times. Remember that you want your heels to have very light contact with the ground throughout the exercise (fig. 7.24a–fig. 7.24b).

After performing the Heel Bounce several times, you're probably wondering why I have you lifting both heels after my warning about the evils of heel lifting in your swing. I have a great reason: it guarantees that you won't lift your

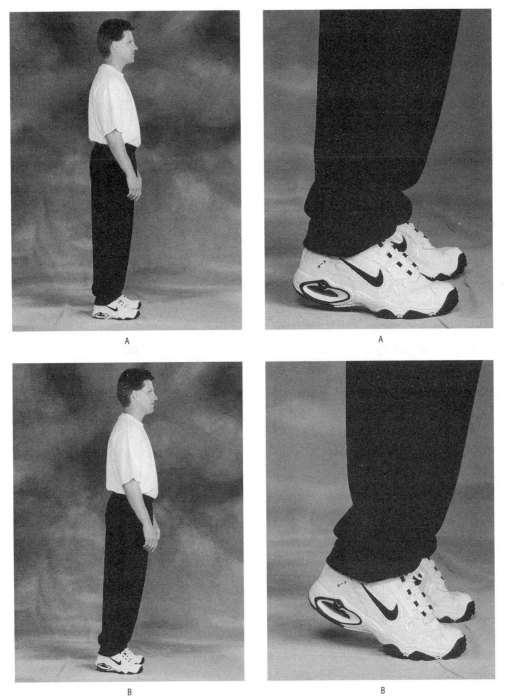

A

A

B

B

FIGURE 7.23 HEEL BOUNCE—SIDE VIEW

FIGURE 7.24 HEEL BOUNCE (CLOSE-UP)—SIDE VIEW

heels—especially your left one—during your swing. As you raise and lower your heels during the routine, you feel your body weight pulling downward, not upward. Your heels feel as if they are reaching for the ground even when you're lifting them. As you lower your heels, the sensation of your weight pulling downward intensifies. That's grounding, simple gravity.

Golfers or martial artists who practice the Heel Bounce become so familiar with the reaction of their body weight being pulled downward that their heels stay put in any movement. It seems like a contradiction that a lift can train you to keep your heels down, but there's really no mystery. The basic martial arts principle of the Heel Bounce is grounding through gravity. In a word, when you apply the principle to your golf swing, your heels will stay down because you have developed a connection with earth power. Remember, the ground is your ultimate leverage point. By befriending it with your downward-centered posture, you'll have the foundation to launch your finest shots.

Body Rotation
That's right—our old Eastern friends Body Rotations I and II can take you on another step to a balanced swing. You have felt how these exercises mimic the correct timing of your arms and body in the golf swing. What is more logical than that they now play a key role in the more advanced mode of your body motion and arm swing? In golfing terms, not much.

Because you have been practicing Body Rotation I, I don't have to show you how to perform it. But, the teacher in me can't help myself. I want to show you not only how each of the exercise's familiar steps applies to your body motion and arm swing, but also how to use the exercise in problem-solving situations. So, here's a quick review:

1. Position your arms up, right arm vertical, left arm horizontal (fig. 7.25a).
2. Keep both hands open, using the V formed by your right thumb and index finger as an aiming sight.
3. Rotate your body to the left, maintaining your arm positions in conjunction with your body (fig. 7.25b–fig. 7.25d).
4. Turn back to the right, keeping the same fixed arm positions (fig. 7.25e–fig. 7.25h).

A

B

C

D

E

F

G

H

Okay, bear with me a moment or two longer about Body Rotation. Here are the key points for our current discussion and for the discussion of problem solving in Chapter 8:

- Your arms and body move in unison—one-piece rotation.
- Your head rotates with your body in both directions.

Again, remember that you are simulating your swing's exact timing.

There is another great reason we're reviewing Body Rotation. It's going to be a part of your Eastern exercise and coordination regimen, one that you will need to practice at least three times a week.

Waving Hands

This Eastern step is the last routine of your stationary exercise program and it truly blends several key elements of your golf swing. In the dojo, I teach it as an intermediate exercise that points the way to more complex moves. The beauty of Waving Hands for the golfer is that it blends weight displacement while it harmonizes your arm motion. So, come on, it's time to "wave."

FIGURE 7.25 BODY ROTATION I—FRONT VIEW

1. Stand with your left leg extended forward and your arms down by your sides (fig. 7.26a). Place your weight equally on both legs.

2. Lift your arms up to your chest, your palms facing down to the ground and your elbows pointed out (fig. 7.26b). Shift most of your weight back onto your right leg.

3. Shift your body straight forward, and extend your arms straight out (fig. 7.26c). Support most of your body weight on your left leg.

4. Move your arms back toward your chest while shifting your weight back onto your right leg (fig. 7.26d–fig. 7.26f). Keep your left leg extended. Repeat this routine ten times.

5. When you have finished, allow your arms to move down to your sides, and distribute your weight evenly on both legs.

Okay, stop for a moment. Let's talk about what just went on with your weight displacement and your arm motions as they relate to your swing. The main focus of this exercise is learning how to move your arms and body in unison. By that, I mean that as your arms extend out, your body weight should shift forward. When your arms retract back to your chest, your body weight shifts back as well. This starts the reconditioning process for your entire body. You are asking your whole body to respond together and flow in one motion, instead of letting multiple parts work against each other.

It's just like when a wave comes in from the ocean—the body of water produces a wave which flows onto the shore. I think that's a great image for this exercise. Your body, or better yet your one-point, is like the ocean, and your arms are like the wave. Neither of them can exist without the other; they are totally interdependent. To make a wave, your body has to be involved, and for the wave to be seen, your arms have to be involved. Be a wave!

Moving Exercises

These exercises represent a dynamic step toward a balanced swing— dynamic as in movement. You want to maintain the fluid exchange of yin and yang that you've injected into your swing. You know how this controlled but explosive power feels, but you want more. You want to feel

A

B

C

D

E

F

FIGURE 7.26 Waving Hands—diagonal view

that smooth flow with every swing. Two moving exercises from my dojo will help keep your body motions and arm swing on course every time you swing the club.

Double Hand Parry

The first moving exercise is one I have developed over the years in my dojo and have found to be a perfect complement to your golf swing. Having discovered that I was blending this martial arts routine into my own swing, I began to think about this unexpected marriage of my martial arts training and golf. I saw, as well as felt, that my own variation of the Double Hand Parry required me to use my arms in a dynamic manner that was carrying over into my golf swing. By this point in my golf career, I had a solid grasp of the traditional swing, but I realized that some of the simplest techniques I had taught in my dojo were strengthening my own Western swing mechanics. Since I was already an accomplished player and this Eastern exercise still helped my game, I figured that the Double Hand Parry could really help struggling golfers locate—or relocate— dynamic movement in their own

swings. I have seen the payoff for my students. The Double Hand Parry delivers when it comes to controlling your arms and body in the golf swing, and it certainly delivers distance and control to your game.

Let's try our first moving exercise.

1. Stand in a normal posture with your hands at your sides (fig. 7.27a).
2. Step out at a 45-degree angle with your left leg while your arms circle up from right to left (fig. 7.27b–fig. 7.27e), your right palm down and your left palm up.
3. Step out with your right foot. Allow your arms to flow downward and over to your right side in a circular motion until they are extended again (fig. 7.27f–fig. 7.27h), your right palm up and your left palm down.
4. Keep stepping and repeating the arm motions for twelve consecutive steps.

Here are three benefits of this exercise that I discovered years ago. They are what you experience after

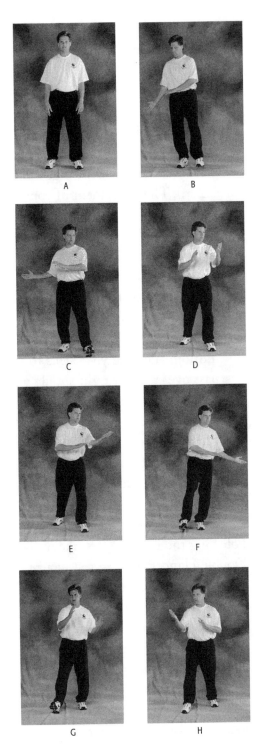

A

B

C

D

E

F

G

H

performing the exercise just a few times:

• Your arms flow in unison with the turning motion of your body. This is exactly how your body should move during your swing.

• The coordinated movement of your arms and body compels you to stay stacked—exactly as you must in your golf swing.

• Your head rotates in unison with your body's rotation, just as it should to defeat any rigidity in your swing.

The big bonus that the Double Hand Parry brings to your swing is that it helps you develop the proper sequencing of your arm motion, body rotation, and even weight transfer. I didn't mention weight transfer until now because I didn't want you to think about it as you were doing the exercise. But, as you perform the routine, your weight shifts with no fuss. That's something you will carry right to the course. I know I did—and still do.

FIGURE 7.27 DOUBLE HAND PARRY—FRONT VIEW

Polishing the Mirror

Polishing the Mirror will be the most difficult exercise from my dojo, but don't panic. I haven't brought you this far on the path of Balanced Golf just to introduce you to an Eastern guide that you will have a hard time following. Relax. Polishing the Mirror might be a little more difficult, but it's still a basic Eastern technique you can master, as long as you use a little patience. For your golf game, the reward for this patience won't be just virtue, but a revelation for fluid movement.

When I first began my training in the martial arts, I learned the original version of Polishing the Mirror, which has been practiced in China for centuries, carefully passed down from master to student. For the golfer, I have broken this exercise down into short sequences that you will combine into a routine of fluid motion.

1. Stand with your arms at chest level, your palms down and your elbows out (fig. 7.28a).
2. Lift your left leg, and slowly turn your body to the right (fig. 7.28b).
3. Extend your left leg forward and stretch your arms outward as you put your foot down (fig. 7.28c).
4. Continue the flow of motion with your arms, and allow them to circle to the left. They should finish up near your left shoulder with your elbows bent (fig. 7.28d). The movement of your arms from beginning to this point should be a half circle.
5. Step forward with your right leg and begin to extend your arms outward (fig. 7.28e–fig. 7.28f).
6. Keep following the circular motion, allowing your arms to pass over to your right shoulder (fig. 7.28g).
7. Repeat the exercise (fig. 7.28a–g) again and again and—well, you get the picture. Practice, practice, practice.

So, what do you get out of Polishing the Mirror? Just like in the Double Hand Parry exercise, you're developing proper sequencing for your arms and body while you're moving. The movement (footwork) itself means that weight transfer, along with moving parts, needs to be negotiated. This is an advanced motion and, to the untrained eye, it looks too simple. But that isn't the

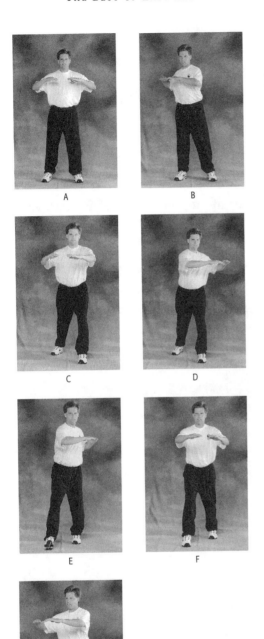

FIGURE 7.28
POLISHING THE
MIRROR—FRONT VIEW

case. To develop perfect unison of your body, arms, and weight transfer, you will need a lot of practice. Unlike the Double Hand Parry exercise, Polishing the Mirror asks that you relax your arms even more, allowing your elbows to fold. The reason for this is to let your ki—your internal energy—flow more easily. If you encourage this type of joint rounding movement, it will affect your whole body, charging you up like a battery. Trust me, it's a powerful and energizing exercise that will give much to your golf game. Just practice it diligently and refined, skilled motion will be yours.

Your Eastern Exercise Regimen

The four stationary and two moving exercises you've just learned are at the heart of Balanced Golf. There are two reasons for this. First, the drills apply to specific parts of your golf game's body motion and arm swing. And, as I will reveal in the next chapter, you can combine these Eastern exercises with Western coordination drills to cure your individual swing flaws. Second, the six Eastern techniques are your personal exercise program. Hopefully, you will practice them at least three times a week. If you do, they will shape up not only your swing but also your flexibility in off-course activities.

Here is your Eastern exercise schedule to golfing success:

Stationary Exercises
Arm Swing—24 repetitions
Heel Bounce—24 repetitions
Body Rotation—24 repetitions
Waving Hands—36 repetitions

Moving Exercises (these should be consecutively in line form)

Double Hand Parry—3 sets of 12
Polishing the Mirror—3 sets of 12

Now, take a deep breath—ki style, of course. You have covered a lot of ground with your Eastern and Western drills. Next, you are about to learn how specific combinations of these drills will tear down any man-made obstacles in your golf swing and make sure they never reappear.

8

POWERFUL PROBLEM SOLVING—
EASTERN AND WESTERN STYLE

When I first meet new students, they're usually breaking laws—the laws of yin and yang, body alignments, fluid movement, or lateral motion. You get the idea. They all come to me with a problem and, more often than not, that problem is excessive body rotation. Perhaps the second most common fault is an out-of-sync arm swing coupled with almost no body motion.

Every step of the way on our path to Balanced Golf, my simple martial arts techniques have distilled physical motion and force into their purest essence, teaching you the most efficient manner in which to move the club. Maximum force out of minimal motion, or pure yin and yang. That's what it's all about—putting together the combination of smoothness and power that players like Freddie Couples possess in their swings.

I have reminded you several times of what the martial artist knows and practices: if one body component moves or turns, so should the others. That's the key to your swing.

Because old patterns of swing movements can be hard to break even when you're working to change them, you sometimes need a little extra help. That's what the Eastern and Western drills in Chapter 7 were and are designed for: to act as your golfing trump card against any swing enemies that might creep back into your swing. Those swing flaws are tough foes. That's the bad news. But the good news, the great news, is that simple combinations of my Eastern and Western drills will chase away these enemies for good and keep you permanently on the path of fluid yin and yang. These blends of East and West are the final physical guides you need to synchronize your swing for maximum fluidity and power. My revolutionary method in merging martial arts and golf drills is the ultimate guide to problem solving in your swing.

SUCCESS STORIES

Before I reveal these simple but amazing combinations of coordination drills, I'll give you an example or two of how well my approach works and of how easy it is. Simplicity of movement, the rule of the dojo, is at the very core of my students' success stories. This Eastern simplicity, along with practice, will make your swing a similar success.

About a year ago, an avid player at the Carolina Country Club—we'll call him Bob—sought my help. Like so many players, Bob loved the game but was totally frustrated with his swing. He told me that he felt as though he never swung the club the same way twice. He couldn't understand why much smaller and less athletic playing partners could hit longer drives than he did.

Just in seeking help, Bob had taken a huge step. He had admitted that something was wrong with his swing, something that he couldn't fix on his own no matter how much he tried. As soon as he had hit a few balls for me, I spotted that all-too-familiar golfing "red flag," excessive body rotation. And because his weekly games of racquetball had ingrained the necessary instincts of kill shots and slams, he was carrying those traits to the golf course. Complicating the rotational problem further was his upper body strength—Bob is a broad-shouldered, thick-chested guy. A powerful build at first glance would seem to be custom-made for long tee shots; however, he was slicing shots badly and losing more distance than anyone else in his group.

As any capable PGA instructor knows, big guys often have the most difficulty in generating a proper rotational move. It's simple anatomy: a broad upper body has more limitations in movement and flexibility. If you think of the most flexible people you know, they all have slim physiques. On the other hand, if someone is heavier, he or she will have restrictions in mobility. This same scenario applies to your golf swing.

Once I got Bob to accept the inherent limitations he had to deal with, he realized that a clear arm swing path with his large upper body was of utmost importance. I had the answers for him to improve. I first taught Bob the principles of the Horse, body alignments, and yin and yang. This whetted his appetite for more. So, after we implemented the basics of these principles, I focused on developing a stacked upper torso and his body motion and arm swing. I told him that we had to zero in on the proper usage of his arms and body—to make sure that they were especially unified during his back-swing and downswing. I pointed out that his tendency was to overpower the golf ball as he did so successfully on the racquetball court. But with this condition in his golf swing, he constantly overtwisted his lower body in the downswing.

What all that meant, I explained, was that he couldn't time the correct arm speed to the rotational motion of his body. Time after time, his arms and miscalculated body rotation meant slices, vicious slices. This lack of unison

violated the fluid exchange of yin and yang energy from his setup to his finish, ruining his impact and decreasing the distance he should have gotten. In the court of golf, when he first came to me, Bob was guilty of violating yin and yang, body alignments, and fluid move-ment. Luckily, I had the perfect rehab program for him—an Eastern drill and a Western drill. Talk about balance.

I began his cure with the One-Foot Drill. As you know, this exer-cise limits the amount of hip rotation you can produce and, more important, you perform this drill with a slower arm speed. I wanted Bob to understand—to feel—that his waist did have some resistance. Because the One-Foot Drill restricted his inclination to twist his body so much, he got the message very quickly. The message was that he could move his upper body and still control his lower body action. With just a few slow swings in the One-Foot stance, he felt his lower body slow down and his timing, or his unison of body motion and arm swing, improved right away.

Once he felt this connection, I showed him the Eastern drill that would balance his arm swing and body motion for good, chipping away the flaw of overrotation. The dojo drill is one you know well—Body Rotation I. To acquire a unified motion with the arms and body in the golf swing, nothing works better than this simple Eastern exercise. And as Bob discovered using a one-piece rotation with the arms and body, the Body Rotation exercise works wonders. In the end, he knocked away the last pieces of an overtwisting body and made his slice history. That's problem solving the East–West way—simple and achievable.

I had another student come to me last year with a fairly common problem. Once again, I put my East–West problem-solving exercises into action. Charles (names have been changed to protect the innocent) suffered from a swing flaw to which most young players fall prey—fast rhythm. This habit has traditionally been one of the hardest for golfers to kick. After many years of playing, Charles couldn't resist swinging from the heels. He could hit long shots with his woods and irons, but they rarely went straight.

He is a big guy, about six foot two and 220 pounds, but I knew that the principles of natural law could harness his raw power if he was willing to listen. When he showed up for our first session, I had him hit twenty shots with his 6-iron. Sure enough, he knocked them a long way, but his shot pattern was all over the place. I stopped him at this point and explained that his major swing flaw was too much arm speed.

I took Charles through the same basics of Balanced Golf from setup to finish that I've shown you throughout this book. Then, we discussed rhythm. I explained what you already know: a fast rhythm usually creates mechanical problems in the transition zone. This was exactly where his problem was located. As his downswing was initiated, he began twisting immediately, producing multiple problems. It made his left leg straighten out very quickly; it was leaving a lot of body weight on his right side; and his hands were unhinging the club prematurely. Not a pretty picture.

I prescribed a combination of two exercises—the Western Long and Slow and the Eastern Waving

Hands. We began with his sand wedge. I had him hit thirty shots with a long backswing and follow-through. Right away, he commented on how rhythmic this exercise was making his swing and on how much more relaxed he felt. Now he didn't feel the urge to lash at the ball.

Once he felt comfortable with the wedge, I moved Charles up to the 7-iron, repeating the same type of shot pattern. Between his shots, as he was setting up over the ball, I would say the key words, "Long and Slow." This painted an image for him and reinforced the physical motions he was trying to imitate. He went on to hit a lot of solid shots in a row, so I had him repeat the exercise with his 3-wood. We went through the same routine. Sure enough, his shots were hit cleanly and flew straight toward the target. At this point, he was very happy with the results but was anxious to hear about his Eastern prescription.

I explained the benefits of Waving Hands and told him what he should be focusing on to improve his swing. The primary purpose was that he now had an exercise to develop proper body and arm connection and a way to feel the inter-nal rhythm of his body. If I could get him to visualize the internal wave of energy within, he could reestablish the proper rhythm of his swing.

We started with the proper sequencing of body and arm motion, focusing on how his body and arms respond together, not independently. Charles got the hang of it, and in a short time was shift-ing body weight and extending his arms as a total unit. I thought he was going to do a backflip, he was so excited. After ten minutes of practice, he was doing the exercise perfectly.

Then I decided to have him pick up his 7-iron again and go through his normal swinging motion, hitting about twenty balls. He was quite surprised to see how quickly the rhythm problem had disappeared and how fluid his swing had become. The balance that was missing in his old Western swing had come alive in his Eastern one.

Charles was thrilled by the turn-around in his game because he was still booming his tee shots farther than his playing partners, but he now had control of his ball. Chalk up another one for Balanced Golf.

EAST-WEST COMBINATIONS

Let's get to the specific combinations of Eastern and Western drills that will help you stay on the path of Balanced Golf. I know that you've learned each drill, but for easy reference I've listed the names here so you don't have to keep thumbing back to Chapter 7. Just refer to this chart, as we go through the proper blending of exercises to solve all your swing emergencies.

WESTERN COORDINATION DRILLS	EASTERN EXERCISES
Half-to-Half Drill	Arm Swinging
Left-Foot Shuffle	Heel Bounce
One-Foot Drill	Body Rotation
Crossing Arms Drill	Waving Hands
Long and Slow Drill	Double Hand Parry
Club the Ball Drill	Polishing the Mirror
Hand Lag Drill	

Now we're going to make sure that you combine the classic Western swing drills with their appropriate Eastern counterparts in addressing your specific swing problems. These examples will give you a reference to match up East and West.

PROBLEM:
Excessive body rotation

SOLUTION:
West—One-Foot Drill
East—Body Rotation

PROBLEM:
Arms-only swing, no body motion

SOLUTION:
West—Left-Foot Shuffle
East—Double Hand Parry
or
West—Half-to-Half Drill
East—Polishing the Mirror

PROBLEM:
Short backswing or follow-through

SOLUTION:
West—Long and Slow Drill
East—Arm Swinging

PROBLEM:
Fast rhythm

SOLUTION:
West—Long and Slow Drill
East—Waving Hands

PROBLEM:
Heels up at impact

SOLUTION:
West—Half-to-Half Drill
East—Heel Bounce

Problem:
Too much wrist action in the backswing or at impact

Solution:
West—Hand Lag Drill
East—Double Hand Parry

Remember, these are just a few examples to get you started. Each of these exercises can be done individually or paired up with its appropriate counterpart. The key is to blend both the East and the West. Then your Balanced Golf swing can appear, giving you all the pars and birdies you've ever wanted.

9

RELAXATION

Calmness is real power. Those four words carry an incredible amount of meaning in the dojo and on the course. No matter how good your swing mechanics may be, the mental part of your game is the glue that holds it all together. I have many students who resist this truth; they have this notion that once they understand the physical moves of a swing, or a kick, or a punch, they have it. They think they can play through anything that disturbs their thoughts. As a result, their mental game takes a backseat to the physical.

Until I had trained in the martial arts for several years, I too bought into this theory. After all, any good instructor tells his students that they must relax to hit the ball properly; however, traditional Western-style instruction mainly preaches relaxation on the physical level.

For a long time in my dojo, I've taught students that attaining the perfect blend of physical movement and emotional focus is like building a house. There are four crucial components: first, the foundation; second, the walls; third, the roof; and fourth, the interior. For my budding martial arts students, I break these four segments down as follows:

• The foundation is your stance—with proper alignments you can perform any technique at a high level.
• The walls represent your limbs. You must become proficient in their use to have good defensive and offensive skills.
• The roof covers and attaches your whole structure. For a martial artist, this element represents the fine-tuning of physical attributes, including speed, timing, distance,

strategies, and environmental awareness.

• The interior represents your emotional development, the unseen forces that dictate either failure or success.

Let's apply the same analogy to your golf swing. Don't take the image too literally when I compare walls to movement. Just look at the broader picture, the picture of your balanced swing. Here's the blueprint to get your golf house in order:

• The foundation represents your setup—the stance that allows you to create your tower of balance for a smooth exchange of yin and yang. Remember, the Horse is a cornerstone of your setup, your foundation.

• The walls are represented by your body motion and arm swing. These two components are the core of your swing and must be synchronized to work as one unit.

• The roof symbolizes your special attributes, including your grip, ball position, swing speed (rhythm), the length of your backswing and follow-through, and even how much weight is transferred during your swing.

• The interior signifies your emotional development, the hidden portion of your swing. If your concentration is constantly being broken or is just underdeveloped, your golf house will surely collapse. Simply put, you must train your mind.

This chapter marks a departure from the rest of the book. We are going to spend almost all of our session in the dojo. Why? Because it's there that you will learn the interior game of Balanced Golf. Within your thoughts, we will plant the Eastern seed of focus that will blossom in your new swing. You have welcomed the physical guides of the East—the Horse stance and other exercises. Now, open your mind to Eastern thought.

In our efforts to chase away rigidity through joint rounding, you learned what physical relaxation means to your game: it freed up your swing for fluid power. You know that if you can feel tightness or physical tension in your muscles, you can round them away.

We are going to take the same approach to your emotional, or interior, game. Mental focus requires much more than simply blocking out bad thoughts long enough to hit a good shot. You can't turn off doubts and anxieties on the course simply by developing a sound swing. Those swing mechanics alone can't do the job. This is where Balanced Golf—truly balanced between the physical and mental game—really does its job, sending you to the tee or green with not only relaxed limbs, but also a relaxed mind.

Somewhere, somehow, you're going to be influenced by negative thoughts. They can take over your swing. Maybe they will make you rush from your transition to down-swing and produce too much rota-tional motion. Maybe they will cause you to grip the club too hard, locking up your limbs for a stiff swing. The variables that mental stress can bring to your swing mechanics are endless—and all bad.

Over the years, two names you've seen time and time again at the top of the leaderboard are Fred Couples and Raymond Floyd. At Augusta, I had the great experience of learning from Raymond what mental focus on the course is all about. When you're paired with him, he eases tension with casual chat, and I discovered something:

his calmness perfectly complements his will to win. I learned that no matter how difficult a lie or how tough a putt, Raymond's calmness allows him to focus only on the shot—not on what can go wrong with it. On those rare occasions when he hits a bad one, he is still able to keep his focus. That's what has helped him beat players who have more classic swings. While I can't promise that a more relaxed mental game will turn you into Raymond Floyd, I can vouch that it will help you beat your weekend partners. Who doesn't want that?

On one particular day I was paired with Raymond, I have to admit that I was nervous. Being fully aware of all his accomplish-ments, I was a bit intimidated. And make no mistake, players of his cali-ber all have the presence of champi-ons. But a funny thing happened as we got into our round. Raymond's casual talk calmed me down. Then, I turned to that Eastern principle I teach in my dojo—calmness is real power. First, through ki's one-point breathing technique, I kept my energy flowing smoothly from my balance center, my abdomen. You already understand how to do this, but in a moment I'm going to expand your knowledge of Eastern breathing patterns. I will introduce you to three of my dojo's meditation techniques that will cleanse your mind of negative energy—fear, doubt, anxiety. They will all evaporate, and you will be left with the full flow and power of a swing your physical Eastern guides have shaped. That's all anyone could need or want on the course, nothing to clutter the path of your swing from setup to finish.

As you practice the Eastern steps for the physical components of your swing, something happens— something besides the dojo's tools of movement guiding you on the course. The more comfortable you become with the physical guides of Balanced Golf, the more important your mental approach, your interior game, becomes. With the exception of introducing ki in your setup, I've focused on your physical skills. That's because you must develop sound mechanics before you can address your mental skills.

If you've gotten this far in the book, you've done that. Now you're ready to design your interior game, to free your swing mechanics from emotional tension. The concept of

clear movement through a clear mind is at the heart of the martial arts. "The mind leads the body," I tell my martial arts students and my golf pupils.

Before a golfer begins the backswing or a martial artist uses a technique, the mind must prepare and command the body into action. Any hesitation or second thought in that command process will ruin the chances for a good swing or self-defense encounter. Your emotional control directs your swing. Any anxiety, anger, or frustration, even too much excitement, will show up in your swing—piling up strokes and decreasing your enjoyment of the game. Also, keep in mind that any emotions you carry to the course will directly affect your physical performance. It's not only those that appear during a round that bother you. Try to eliminate preexisting bad energy as well.

This is where three of my dojo's most powerful—perhaps the most powerful—techniques will teach you how your mind leads your body. These easy-to-follow basic breathing patterns, meditations, and energy drill will complete your path to Balanced Golf.

EASTERN BREATHING PATTERNS

You have already been training your ki breathing patterns; we discussed them in the very first chapter. Even though I know you're completely familiar and comfortable with these two breathing patterns, it's necessary for me to take you through them again at this point, just as I do my students at each training session.

Activating Your One-Point

1. Place your hand two inches below your navel; this is your one-point (fig. 9.1). Leave your hand on the spot (fig. 9.2a). Feel free to tap the spot several times as when you first performed the routine. The light taps activate your one-point more easily. You will feel the slight, familiar tingling and warmth that you always feel when your one-point is activated.
2. Inhale through your nose, and feel the rush of air enter your body and expand your lower abdominal area (fig. 9.2b).
3. Exhale slowly through your mouth, moving your one-point

FIGURE 9.1 FINDING YOUR ONE-POINT—FRONT VIEW

inward toward your spine (fig. 9.2c). Breathe out completely. You should feel a relaxed sensation spreading from your one-point to the rest of your body—easing all your stiffness from head to toe. If you feel warmth throughout your body or experience a relaxed heaviness in your limbs, these are positive signs of greater awareness and progress.

A　　　　　　　　　　　B　　　　　　　　　　　C

FIGURE 9.2 BREATHING FROM YOUR ONE-POINT—SIDE VIEW

One-point breathing is half the pie when it comes to breathing development. Now, follow along to the Visual Breathing exercise, and you can have the rest of your pie.

Visual Breathing

This breathing technique will complete your understanding of breath control. The Visual Breathing exercise plays an integral role in your progression because it provides you with a physical gauge—your arms—to monitor your inhalation and exhalation.

1. Stand with your feet shoulder-width apart and your arms down by your sides (fig. 9.3a).
2. Inhale, expanding your one-point, and raise your arms (palms up), until they are above your head (fig. 9.3b–fig. 9.3c).
3. As you exhale evenly, lower your arms in front of your body, your palms facing each other (fig. 9.3d–fig. 9.3f). Remember to exhale as deeply as possible, feeling your one-point contract inward.

FIGURE 9.3 VISUAL BREATHING—FRONT VIEW

By using this breathing pattern you are not only relaxing for your swing but also clearing your mind of stressful thoughts and emotions.

Now that you've felt the internal energy of ki flowing from your breathing exercises, it's time to incorporate your last two teachers—meditation and an energy drill. In fact, the reason I've waited to reveal these two elements is because you must have some experience in breath control to use them. You see, breath control is the bridge for your mind and body. It influences both and connects them for all your actions. If you have proper control of your breath, it calms you physically and emotionally. It also gives you the ability to make clear decisions and stay in the present moment. That means your mind will not be cluttered with too many thoughts. So, proper regulation of your breathing cycle is very important, and it will even aid you in your upcoming meditations. Learn to breathe deeply and evenly, and your bridge will be solid as a rock.

MARTIAL ARTS MEDITATIONS FOR YOUR GOLF GAME

The simple meditation techniques I will show you in this section open the doorway to your mind. I know, this sounds like a line from a movie or a self-help guru. But whether I'm teaching these methods to a golfer or a martial artist, the applications are similar in nature. That nature is contained within the proverb of "Mind of No Mind," or what the Japanese refer to as *mushin*. It is said that achieving this state of mind is the ultimate—and I can tell you first-hand that this is a truism. By attaining a mind of no thought, you respond instinctively rather than with your Western mind's analysis.

There's nothing dark or even mystical about basic Eastern meditations. They are simple steps that anyone can use to achieve astounding results. The outcome is dependant on your desire and goals—the more you put into it, the greater the results. As one of my master teachers once said, "Anything of value in your training takes great effort and continued practice."

You may be wondering what force the martial artist taps into during meditation. Simply put, it's energy circulation. We all have internal rivers of energy within our bodies, and they are really responsible for maintaining our existence. Not to get too obscure, but from an Eastern viewpoint these circuits of energy give you life, and if one of them is disrupted or blocked you become ill. By using proper meditation exercises, you can keep these rivers flowing properly and can stay in a balanced state emotionally and physically.

Sometimes when I first mention Eastern circulation to golfers, they look puzzled. But when I explain that energy circulation is the life force that exists within you, in your interior, and that it can influence the negative emotions that block the doorway to your mind, they listen. If you can just welcome these Eastern meditations into your Western game as friends, I guarantee they won't let you down.

To meditate properly, you need a quiet spot. You will need someplace where the phone won't ring, the television's off, and there are no other distractions. By establishing your own area of calmness, you will achieve better results and find a stillness inside of you much quicker.

I have told you to keep your distractions to a minimum, but you can use a radio or a CD player softly. Music can be soothing and very useful in your meditation sessions. However, once again your selection is important—don't choose rock 'n' roll or any songs that have lyrics. They're too distracting, and your mind will constantly wander. If you stop by your local music store, I'm confident you'll find an appropriate selection. Look in the Instrumental or New Age areas. They always have a great assortment, and any of these will work quite well.

When some of my martial arts and golf students begin meditating, they think that by simply closing their eyes and taking deep breaths, they're meditating. They're close, but there's still much more to be incorporated. That's why I just went over your one-point breathing technique. Proper meditation requires you to tune into the expansion and contraction of your breaths. Because your breathing patterns are affected by whatever emotions you're experiencing, controlling them is vital to the martial artist or the golfer. In the dojo, if you panic or feel anxiety when executing techniques, there's a high probability of failure. A skilled opponent will detect your uneasiness and exploit this weakness. Another thing is certain as well: if you lose control for a moment, your breathing pattern will be disturbed, and that means your emotional control will deteriorate. If you can't keep an even frame of mind, you simply can't produce the type of energy you need for powerful, fluid movement.

We are at the key question: what does Eastern meditation mean to you, the golfer? I'm not going to deny that high-level meditation techniques tap into spiritual forces as well as energy circulation. But, for the golfer, a simple understanding of meditation is all that's needed. All your life you've known that your mind instinctively relays thoughts, emotions, and anxieties into physical feelings. Have your hands ever shaken just a bit when you're nervous? When you've been excited, has it ever felt like your heart's pounding against your chest? These are the kinds of things that a

golfer has to be able to control. Shaky hands caused by nerves will certainly affect your swing or your putt. And if your heart's pounding, you're more than likely going to make some sort of swing error. Either way, a mishit is on the way, and all because your interior game is sending the wrong signals to your physical game. The key to successful golf meditation is to block out disturbing thoughts—at the very least it should be long enough to take a fluid swing. In the dojo, we call this mental state *unattachment*. That's your goal.

Right now, you probably think that your oversized titanium driver is still your biggest weapon. You're wrong. Unattachment, developed through meditation, is your ultimate weapon.

Meditation 1: Absorbing Your Power

In my dojo, I teach Meditation 1 as they do in the Chinese tradition. This stance is called the *Wuji* position. Wuji is considered the absorbing posture. It teaches you to absorb energy into your body, developing a connection with earth power.

The first step in developing internal energy is to fill yourself. By doing so, you'll have an extra reserve of power to send out whenever you need it. This is great for your golf stance and swing because this force will last your whole round.

Now, it's time to establish your Wuji stance. Prepare to fill up.

Wuji Inhalation

1. Stand with your feet shoulder-width apart and your arms slightly rounded away from your sides.
2. Bend your knees slightly.
3. Your head must be level, your eyes looking straight ahead.
4. I suggest that you close your eyes halfway. This helps create a relaxed feeling.
5. Begin to inhale, trying to imagine a wave or wind of energy circulating at your feet. I know it sounds somewhat mysterious, but attaching this visual image with your breathing is very important.
6. Continue inhaling as deeply as you can manage. By now you should have the sensation of energy circulating from the soles of your feet, up into your legs, into your torso, and then up to the base of your neck.

FIGURE 9.4 WUJI STANCE—FRONT VIEW

FIGURE 9.5 WUJI STANCE—SIDE VIEW

It may take you some time to develop a strong sensation of energy flowing throughout your body. However, if you continue the practice and are disciplined, you can do it.

7. Once you've breathed in as deeply as possible, pause for a moment.

Wuji Exhalation

1. Begin to exhale. As you do, imagine the energy now flowing down into your shoulders, arms, and forearms and out of your hands, letting it shoot out of your fingertips like a water hose.
2. Exhale completely and pause at the end.
3. Repeat the entire inhalation and exhalation process.

The more you practice this posture, the better it will feel. And you know what? Your awareness of traveling energy within your body will get even better. Because your Wuji stance and one-point breathing have been combined, your emotional road bumps are smoothed out. You have attained that momentary void when peaceful feelings filter into every part of your body. For the golfer, this means the negative thoughts that can cause hesitation and overanalyzing are now dissolved and sent out of your body.

Meditation 2: Circling Your Power

Meditation 2 takes your understanding and control of energy circulation a step further. In the dojo, we refer to this stance as the *circling* posture. This meditation takes the energy you've brought upward into your body, and teaches you to move it in a circle around your upper torso and arms. By learning this skill, you'll develop the ability to move energy within your own body.

1. Begin with a stance that has your feet spaced at shoulder width.
2. Position your arms in front of your body, and imagine that you're holding a large ball. Your fingertips should be about six inches apart. Keep your shoulders and elbows relaxed (fig. 9.6–fig. 9.7).
3. Activate your one-point and begin inhaling deeply.
4. Focus on your internal energy, letting it flow in your left arm.

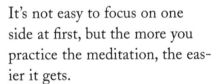

FIGURE 9.6 Circling posture—front view

FIGURE 9.7 Circling posture—side view

It's not easy to focus on one side at first, but the more you practice the meditation, the easier it gets.

5. Continue inhaling, letting the energy flow from your left arm into your shoulders and across to your right arm. Your energy is circling.

6. As you complete your inhalation, your energy reaches your right hand. That's one cycle.

Once you finish inhaling, start exhaling and move your energy around once again. After some time, you'll even *feel* the energy travel from the fingertips of your right hand over into the fingertips of your left hand. Don't be alarmed; that's a good sign.

You should make an entire circle with each inhalation and exhalation. I know it may be difficult for you to visualize the energy traveling at first, but with persistent training you'll develop an awareness—and the results will amaze you.

Meditation 3: Extending Your Power

In my dojo, I teach this meditation technique to ensure that students are mentally prepared to extend and finish all their techniques. I have also discovered that this meditation is a perfect tool to train the golfer's mind to extend energy throughout the swing.

Before you begin this technique, you have to be completely comfortable with Meditations 1 and 2. You must be able to summon that warm or tingling surge of energy by activating your one-point breathing. If you're not yet able to do this, don't worry. You haven't failed some test. After all, you've absorbed nearly all of the steps of Balanced Golf. There's no stress here; Meditations 1 and 2 are about relaxation. All you have to do is return to your quiet area and perform our first two postures a little more. It's no different than choosing to hit a few more buckets of balls at the driving range. Practice does make perfect—an old saying, but true nonetheless.

A few more meditation sessions later, and you will be feeling the flow of warm circular energy. Congratulations, you're ready for Meditation 3.

1. Assume a stance with your feet spread shoulder-width apart.
2. Raise your arms up in front of your body and extend them forward, your fingers up and your palms facing out (fig. 9.8–fig. 9.9). Your hands should be about six inches apart. Your fingertips should be at eye level.
3. Begin inhaling and, just as in Meditations 1 and 2, move that now-familiar rush of warm energy up from the soles of your feet and into your legs and upper torso, ending at the base of your neck.
4. Once you finish inhaling deeply, pause for a moment.
5. Exhale and split your energy down both sides of your body. It should flow from your shoulders, down your arms, and out of both hands. You can focus on the energy shooting out from the middle of your palms or out of your fingertips. Either one is acceptable.

FIGURE 9.8 EXTENDING POSTURE—FRONT VIEW

FIGURE 9.9 EXTENDING POSTURE—SIDE VIEW

Meditation 3 is an advanced posture, but with continuous practice you'll see the value. Once you've mastered it, sending that energy out of your body and into the club will become second nature.

Remember to practice all three meditations in the order that I've laid them out. For instance, it's important that you don't begin with Meditation 3. Why? Because you'll be using up all of your own energy. You need to start with Meditation 1 and absorb some first—this will give you an extra reserve to tap.

Also, if you intend to practice all three meditations in one session, break them up into equal time limits. For example, allow five minutes for each meditation. This will ensure a proper balance and actually accelerate your internal development.

Your mind is really leading your body and swing now. Here's what each meditation is doing and will do for your swing throughout your future rounds:

- Meditation 1 absorbs energy, filling you with the internal power your swing will use.
- Meditation 2 begins the energy circulation process, developing an awareness so that internal energy can be transformed into physical energy.
- Meditation 3 extends your energy, allowing you to use your internal and external energy together.

With the combined effort of these three meditations, you will certainly reap the benefits of reduced stress, more clarity in your decision making, and an ease of movement. They are your ultimate interior guides. Follow them, and your swing will never collapse from within.

Now, you're going to meet your final Eastern relaxation guide. This training exercise will greet you in a surprising way, but in a familiar place—the dojo.

EASTERN ENERGY DRILL: FEELING RELAXED POWER

You are about to experience what truly relaxed power can and should feel like. This energy drill is commonly called Push Hands and is performed with a partner. It comes from the martial arts teachings of China. However, there are many systems throughout the world that use variations of this exercise. All of them key in on one objective: by using this type of training method, you isolate a realistic way to feel relaxed muscles. If you are tense or firm up your muscular structure during this exercise, you're going to know it. And that's important feedback to you. It's a learning process, and by doing this drill over and over, you'll develop the relaxed power of a skilled martial artist.

Now, grab a training partner and follow along as you discover true relaxation. First, let's get the stance down.

1. Stand with your partner face-to-face and about an arm's length apart (fig. 9.10). Extend your left leg forward.

FIGURE 9.10 PUSH HANDS STANCE—DIAGONAL VIEW

all of your body and arm alignments correct, so double-check your positions. Now, let's push hands:

1. Move your arms straight forward and push into your partner (fig. 9.11a–fig. 9.11c). Your body weight shifts forward as well. Your partner yields to this surge of energy by moving backward slightly.

2. After your arms have extended, start circling them to the right (fig. 9.11d–fig. 9.11e). This is the forward-most position of your body and arms. Eighty percent of your weight is on your left leg. Remember this: 80 percent of your weight has shifted to your left leg. Sound familiar? It should. That's what you've been doing in your swing's follow-through and finish.

3. Continue moving your arms to the right following a circular motion. The whole circling pattern of your arms is about fifteen inches wide. As you reach the right side of your circle, retract your arms and allow your partner to push into you (fig. 9.11f). Let your body weight shift back onto your right leg as

2. Place your left hand to the side of and under your partner's right elbow.

3. Place your right hand on the outside of your partner's right wrist. Your right palm faces up.

4. Your partner positions his or her hands exactly as you've positioned yours.

5. Make sure that your weight is equal on both legs. Now you're grounded.

That's your starting stance for Push Hands. It's important to have

you yield to your partner's motions. There should be no resistance in your arms to stop the forward pressure of your partner—you're just yielding and guiding the incoming force.

4. Your arms and body move back to their original position (fig. 9.11g). But don't stop—keep moving through the exercise.

You must practice Push Hands in multiple repetitions. Instead of thinking of how many arm circles you have to make, set a time limit. I would suggest at least five minutes for beginners. Once you feel comfortable with the exercise, work your way up to fifteen minutes.

While you are going through the drill, just let your body weight rock back and forth while you extend and retract your relaxed arms. There should be a unison of motion while you're pushing and retreating. With the push, as your weight gradually shifts, your arms gradually extend. As you retreat, your weight slowly shifts back, and your arms slowly circle back to your chest.

Remember that you and your partner should have fun with Push Hands. It's not a competition to

FIGURE 9.11 PUSH HANDS EXERCISE— DIAGONAL VIEW

find out who can push harder or knock the other person off balance, not even in the dojo. If you're trying to push your partner through a wall, the drill has no value. Your focus should be on reading the incoming force and learning how to redirect it.

The Push Hands energy drill provides many valuable tools for the golfer:

• It teaches how your muscles should be relaxed as your weight shifts forward and backward, feeling the connection with earth power. You should not have any tension in your legs or upper torso—only fluid movement. After you go through the exercise several times, you realize how much easier it is to do when you're using your body, not just relying on the strength of your arms. Just like a golf swing.

• The drill teaches you that when you extend and retract your arms, your muscles should feel relaxed and, at a certain level, soft. By maintaining a slight bend in your arms, creating a joint rounding effect, you will have an easier time staying relaxed. You know that a fully extended arm has tension and rigidity.

• Developing proper unison of the body and arms during this exercise is a valuable tool. By developing an awareness of body and arm connection when you're pushing, you're promoting a total body response. It's up to you to make sure that both are being used together with a balance between them.

Congratulations. You've absorbed, circled, and extended energy. You've felt relaxed power. If you practice these training methods on a regular basis, I promise you will see great results. The combination of these exercises is so powerful that your mind and body will become One, making you feel more at ease during crucial strategy decisions and analysis of swing flaws. In the end, that will mean lower scores and more satisfaction on your part.

At this point, I have to applaud you and your efforts. You're there—you've achieved Balanced Golf. You know the Eastern mechanics from setup to finish. You know how to keep them on track. And your guides from the dojo have brought your game the power and control you were anticipating. If you keep your commitment level up, all your goals will be fulfilled.

Listen to your Eastern guides, and practice their teachings. They will never let you down. Need proof? Just look at those long, straight shots. Just feel how fluid and effortless your swing is now. Whatever happened to those hooks and slices? They have vanished, courtesy of basic martial arts principles. Just look at those strokes falling off your handicap. You only have one thing left to do: keep your game pointed to the East, the home of Balanced Golf.

10

THE GOLDEN RULES OF BALANCED GOLF

The following rules are a consolidated list of Balanced Golf principles. Use them as your quick reference guide and reminders.

- Your body motion and arms must dominate your swing. This creates a fluid exchange of yin and yang energy.
- Eastern joint rounding eases away rigidity in your swing, supplying you with fluid movement and power.
- The natural law of lateral motion empowers your body to move to the right in your backswing and over to the left in your downswing.
- Maintain the stacked body alignments of your upper torso and lower body throughout the swing.

- The hinging and unhinging motion of your wrists must be done gradually.
- Lateral motion—not rotational motion—must start your downswing.
- Eastern and Western coordination drills keep your body motion and arm swing in proper form. With continued use, your physical skills will stay finely tuned.
- Synchronize your power sources; they should all release together.
- Power comes from the ground up.
- Training the body is not enough—you must train the mind. Use the one-point breathing patterns, Eastern

meditations, and Eastern energy drill to develop your interior, your mind.

- Your mind leads your body and the swing. Positive commands from your mind will send the appropriate messages to your body.

- *Practice, practice, practice* your Eastern techniques.

GLOSSARY OF EASTERN TERMS

BODY ALIGNMENTS. A principle that utilizes optimum positions for your limbs, lower body, upper torso, and head. This theory helps you create maximum power with no strain on your body.

DOJO. A martial arts academy

EARTH POWER. A principle that demonstrates the effectiveness of grounded power. A golfer should root and absorb force from the ground up, developing a very stable base.

JOINT ROUNDING. The relaxed, supple state your joints should maintain to minimize tension in your body. It also assists with the flow of your internal energy.

KI PRINCIPLES. A series of principles that unify your physical and emotional energies. Once devel-oped, your internal power is greatly magnified.

MEDITATIONS. A method for you to develop relaxation and mind clar-ity, both of which will help you to perform at your highest level

NATURAL LAW. The physical and emotional truths that govern our bodies

NEW MOTIONS. A principle that teaches you to learn new physical movements in an exaggerated form. By using long and wide actions, you master all the nuances of precise motion.

ONE-POINT. A point that is two inches below your navel. It is the balance center from which all of your golf game's physical, mental, and emotional characteristics emanate and the center from which you control your breathing patterns from your setup to your finish.

YANG ENERGY. Movement that creates any degree of force

YIN ENERGY. Movement that is passive and yielding in nature. In application, it occurs just before and just after forceful movement.

INDEX

Snead, Sam, 58
Speed, 107–8, 111–13
   arm swing and, 136–38
   of arms, 109, 113–14
   impact and, 78
   transition and, 61
Square clubface, 41–43
Stack
   in backswing, 45
   in finish, 101
   in impact, 82
   in setup, 19–21
Stance, 187, 188
   strength of. *See* Strength of stance
   width of, 7
Stationary exercises, 165–72, 178
Straight arm punch, 119
Strange, Curtis, 65
Strength of stance
   in backswing, 44
   in transition, 65–67
Swing. *See* Arm swing; Backswing;
   Golf swing
Swing center, 7–8
Swing exercise, 21–24
Swing path, 136
   target line for, 138–41
Swing surge, 60

Takeaway, 73
Target line, 138–41
Ten Golden Rules of Balanced Golf,
   207–8
Timing, 109

Top of backswing, 38–43
   clubface in, 41–43
   knee flex in, 38
   left arm in, 39–41
   right elbow in, 39
   shaft aligment in, 43
   waist bend in, 39
Transition, 55–72
   body alignment in, 58–59
   Eastern, 59–72
   hip girdle in, 78
   joint rounding in, 62–65
   knees in, 58
   left arm and lag in, 57
   left heel in, 57–58
   strength of stance in, 65–67
   Western, 55–59
   yin and yang in, 12, 59–62, 73
Trevino, Lee, 7, 43

Unattachment, 196
Unbendable Arm, 47
Upper torso
   in downswing, 133
   in finish, 97
   link with arms in arm swing,
    141–44
   as power source, 108, 109, 111–13

Vaughn, Mo, 112
Visual breathing, 29–31, 192–94

Waist bend
   in impact, 79